Benchmark Tasks for Job Analysis
A Guide for Functional Job Analysis (FJA) Scales

SERIES IN APPLIED PSYCHOLOGY

Edwin A. Fleishman, George Mason University
Series Editor

Psychology in Organizations: Integrating Science and Practice
Kevin R. Murphy and Frank E. Saal

Teamwork and the Bottom Line: Groups Make a Difference
Ned Rosen

Patterns of Life History: The Ecology of Human Individuality
Michael D. Mumford, Garnett Stokes, and William A. Owens

Work Motivation
Uwe Kleinbeck, Hans-Henning Quast, Henk Thierry, and Harmut Häcker

Human Error: Cause, Prediction, and Reduction
John W. Senders and Neville P. Moray

Contemporary Career Development Issues
Robert F. Morrison and Jerome Adams

Personnel Selection and Assessment: Individual and Organizational Perspectives
Heintz Schuler, James L. Farr, and Mike Smith

Justice in the Workplace: Approaching Fairness in Human Resource Management
Russell Cropanzano

Organizational Behavior: The State of the Science
Jerald Greenberg

Police Psychology Into the 21st Century
Martin I. Kurke and Ellen M. Scrivner

Benchmark Tasks for Job Analysis: A Guide for Functional Job Analysis (FJA) Scales
Sidney A. Fine and Maury Getkate

Benchmark Tasks for Job Analysis
A Guide for Functional Job
Analysis (FJA) Scales

Sidney A. Fine
Sidney A. Fine Associates

Maury Getkate
Royal Canadian Mounted Police

LEA
LAWRENCE ERLBAUM ASSOCIATES, PUBLISHERS
1995   Mahwah, New Jersey

Lawrence Erlbaum Associates, Inc., Publishers
10 Industrial Avenue
Mahwah, New Jersey 07430

Cover design by Cheryl Minden

Library of Congress Cataloging-in-Publication Data

Fine, Sidney A., 1915–
    Benchmark tasks for job analysis : a guide for functional job
analysis (FJA) scales / by Sidney A. Fine and Maury Getkate.
        p. cm.
    Includes bibliographical references and index.
    ISBN 0-8058-1813-8 (alk. paper).—ISBN 0-8058-1814-6
    1. Job analysis. I. Getkate, Maury. II. Title.
    HF5549.5.J6F56 1995
    658.3'06—dc20   95-20248
                                                          CIP

Books published by Lawrence Erlbaum Associates are printed on
acid-free paper, and their bindings are chosen for strength and
durability.

Printed in the United States of America
10 9 8 7 6 5 4 3 2 1

To Marilyn

and

To Lilian, Dara, and Kevin

Contents

Foreword

Edwin A. Fleishman
George Mason University

There is a compelling need for innovative approaches to the solution of many pressing problems involving human relationships in today's society. Such approaches are more likely to be successful when they are based on sound research and applications. The Series in Applied Psychology offers publications that emphasize state-of-the-art research and its application to important issues of human behavior in a variety of social settings. The objective is to bridge both academic and applied interests.

Sidney Fine has been one of the pioneers in the field of industrial/organizational psychology concerned with conceptualizing and describing the tasks that people perform in the workplace. In this book, Fine and Getkate are making a very strong assertion—namely that a primary objective of industrial/organizational psychology needs to be the comprehensive description of work tasks in ways that satisfy the needs of the organization for staffing, training, compensation, career planning, and job design. In my earlier book, *Taxonomies of Human Performance: The Description of Human Tasks* (with Marilyn Quaintance), I tried to show the centrality of human tasks to our understanding of human behavior and the need for generalizable constructs in this domain of study. In our book, Quaintance and I compared alternative ways of describing human tasks and stressed how the purpose of the task analysis shapes the kinds of constructs and descriptions that are most appropriate. Prominent among the job analysis systems discussed in our book was the Functional Job Analysis (FJA) system developed by Fine.

Fine has been one of our most persistent investigators concerned with the language of job analysis. He has pointed out that the level of analysis is crucial, and that jobs can be studied at the occupation, job, duty, task element, or critical incident level. In this book, Fine and Getkate make the case for the use of tasks as the appropriate level of analysis of work requirements. Because tasks are not natural isolates that stand alone ("like organisms"), they need to be captured by analysis. The conceptual framework and method of analysis advocated is that of FJA, a methodology that Fine first conceived and developed in the 1960s. In this book, Fine and Getkate have described the method in great detail and have provided benchmark tasks from a wide array of occupations to aid practitioners in using it.

FJA has been the basis of the national occupational classification systems in the United States and Canada for a generation. It is also in use in many industries and by governments in Europe and Asia. It is our belief that this book and its periodic updating can serve as a basic reference for communication and research among human resource practitioners and industrial/organizational psychologists. This book fills the need for a practical guide to the use of this important approach to job analysis.

Preface

This book is the product of a lifetime of study, work, and collaboration with colleagues, clients, and workers. As an avid student, I have been nurtured on the literature of industrial and organizational psychology, the sociology of work, and on systems theory and thinking.

However, since I ventured to explore work as a manifestation of human functional behavior almost a half century ago, I had to break new ground. The literature of job analysis hardly existed. The functional concepts I was proposing had some analogues in other fields such as biology but were only a glimmer in psychology. There was not even a proper vocabulary to draw on. On the whole, it was a lonely undertaking.

ACKNOWLEDGMENTS

Support and encouragement for my exploration came from my mentor at George Washington University, James C. Mosel, whose brilliance illuminated my path. Two of my colleagues at the U.S. Employment Service were also especially supportive and helpful, A. Bennett Eckerson and Jewell Boling.

More recently, my thinking has been sharpened, refined, and enriched by interaction with Professor Steven Cronshaw of the University of Guelph, Ontario, Canada, and my co-author, Maury Getkate. Over the years, I have been extraordinarily fortunate in my professional associations, among them Edwin A. Fleishman and Richard C. Bolles, gaining many insights from my conversations with them. I am extremely grateful to those whom

I have named as well as the dozens of unnamed persons who have enriched
my professional life and helped me grow.

Sidney A. Fine

—DISK ORDERING INFORMATION—

The benchmark tasks are available on a 3½" DOS computer disk for speedier
reference and for entering and comparing your own tasks for a particular
scale and level. To order the disk, send your name, address, and phone
number to Lawrence Erlbaum Associates, 10 Industrial Avenue, Mahwah,
New Jersey 07430, attention Order Department. Please enclose a check for
$1.00, including postage and handling, and allow 4 weeks for receipt of disk.

Chapter **1**

Job Analysis and Benchmarks

JOB ANALYSIS IS ESSENTIAL TO FULFILL MANY ORGANIZATIONAL OBJECTIVES

Human resource management is currently the stylish label attached to what has formerly been known as "personnel" or "personnel operations." What it refers to is an organization's activities, among others, to select, hire, appraise performance, pay, promote, and transfer workers.

These activities have two primary purposes. The organization wants to secure an efficient and effective (productive) workforce—the best it can get for what it wants to spend, and it wants to deal with its workforce in a fair and equitable manner for both morale and legal reasons. What is good for morale is believed to contribute to being productive. And certainly staying within the law is a good way to keep out of trouble. All of these activities and their worthy objectives involve a lot of technical work, the underpinning for all of them being objective, detailed descriptions about the work that needs to get done. Obtaining the information for these descriptions is job analysis.

This volume deals with a method of job analysis especially designed to obtain and communicate information about jobs. Specifically, we describe the procedures involved in developing information about job tasks, evaluating their relevance to job performance, and utilizing this information in job evaluation.

LANGUAGE: A FUNDAMENTAL PROBLEM IN JOB ANALYSIS

Gathering job analysis information that is detailed, objective, reliable, and valid (these are the holy cows of the art and science of industrial psychology) might seem to be simple, but it is not. Regardless of the method used to convey job analysis information, it is still descriptive information

1

conveyed by means of language. Verbs are used to denote actions; nouns to denote material, products, subject matter, and services, as well as machines, tools, equipment, and work aids. Sometimes adverbs and adjectives slip in to emphasize one or another action, material, or tool to indicate standards or to suggest degrees of efficiency and effectiveness.

Left to their own devices, respondents, whether incumbents or analysts, introduce subjective elements into the descriptive material. They have a world of words to choose from, and one observer's choice may not be that of another. This calls the reliability and validity of the observations into question. It is inherently very difficult to choose words that reflect the relative differences in complexity among the work requirements of various jobs. Yet this is what needs to be done if the objectives of fairness and equality are to be realized in carrying out the activities previously listed. Because we are dealing with words that have a strong subjective element, human resource personnel are driven to make assumptions and inferences that weaken the validity of the data. Functional Job Analysis (FJA) has been designed to deal directly with this problem and thus produce more objective descriptive data. How it does this is described in what follows. Benchmarks are the capstone of this effort.

FJA CONTROLS THE LANGUAGE OF JOB ANALYSIS

The main thrust of FJA is to tackle the language of job description and to control its use so various observers can produce data about jobs all can agree on. The following are some of the ways in which FJA controls the use of language:

- FJA uses the natural dimensionality inherent in the English language as a point of departure. All this means is that by studying how words have been commonly used descriptively one finds some words have been naturally clustered to express a hierarchy of complexity or skill, for example, *feed*, *tend*, *operate*, and *setup* machines imply a successively greater degree of involvement and hence skill on the part of the worker.
- FJA draws a sharp distinction between the verbs used to describe what workers do and what gets done. For example, a verb such as *welding* tells what is getting done. It can be done by a worker "operating" a machine or "manipulating" welding tools. Similarly, a verb such as *reporting* tells what is being accomplished, but it is important to distinguish whether the worker is "compiling" data for the report, "analyzing" the data for optional interpretations, or "coordinating" the data to make recommendations. These different

ways of functioning with regard to an output can have important implications for personnel operations.

- FJA recognizes that the objects of worker behaviors can be Things, Data, or People and there needs to be a coherence, a matching, between the action verbs used and the results of those actions. For example, verbs associated with Thing actions need to have Thing outputs.
- FJA insists that describing the work that gets done and what workers do needs to avoid the use of qualifying adjectives and adverbs. Adverbs and adjectives need to be restricted to describe performance standards.
- FJA uses a basic English sentence to describe tasks. A task performed by a worker must include an action verb and an indication of the object of the action (Thing, Data, or People); using what Tools, Machines, Equipment, or Work Aids; drawing on what knowledge and instructions; relying on what skills and abilities; in order to achieve/produce what.

These considerations and specific limitations serve as controls in the use of language to describe work and serve to clarify the language of description and the elements linking job requirements and worker qualifications.

THE ROLE OF FJA SCALES

The language controls are made possible through the use of seven scales, each of which is a channel for the language customarily used to describe what workers do in jobs. For example, workers physically relate to things, mentally relate to data, interpersonally relate to people. Three scales take the behavioral terms used to express these relationships, define them, and organize them from lowest to highest complexity as shown in Fig. 1.1.

These scales plus four others are ordinal, meaning the levels of the scales go from low to high with the higher including the lower levels. They are used to evaluate and rate the specific descriptive material of jobs and produce comparative ratings on each of 10 components—three for levels of difficulty and three for orientation to Things, Data, and People—and four for levels of Worker Instructions, Reasoning, Math, and Language (see Appendix A).

The result is a conceptual framework that anyone, but especially the job analyst, can consult to understand and establish the level of complexity that may be associated with a task. An effect of language control is to generate a terminology for "what workers do" and a terminology for "what gets

THINGS | DATA | PEOPLE

High

THINGS
4a. Precision Working
b. Setting Up
c. Operating-Controlling II

DATA
6. Synthesizing
5a. Innovating
b. Coordinating

PEOPLE
7. Mentoring
6. Negotiating
5. Supervising

Medium

THINGS
3a. Manipulating
b. Operating-Controlling I
c. Driving-Controlling
d. Starting Up

2a. Machine Tending I
b. Machine Tending II

DATA
4. Analyzing
3a. Computing
b. Compiling

PEOPLE
4a. Consulting
b. Instructing
c. Treating

3a. Sourcing Information
b. Persuading
c. Coaching
d. Diverting

Low

THINGS
1a. Handling
b. Feeding-Offbearing

DATA
2. Copying
1. Comparing

PEOPLE
2. Exchanging Information
1a. Taking Instructions-Helping
b. Serving

FIG. 1.1. Summary chart of worker function scales.

NOTES:

1. Each hierarchy is independent of the other. It would be incorrect to read the functions across the three hierarchies as related because they appear to be on the same level. The definitive relationship among functions is within each hierarchy, not across hierarchies. Some broad exceptions are made in the next note.

2. Data is central since a worker can be assigned even higher data functions across the three hierarchies as related because level of their respective scales. This is not so for Things and People functions. When a Things function remain at the lowest Precision Working), the Data function is likely to be at least Compiling or Computing. When a People function is at the fourth level (e.g., Consulting, the Data function is likely to be at least Analyzing and possibly Innovating or Coordinating. Similarly for Supervising and Negotiating, Mentoring in some instances can call for Synthesizing.

3. Each function in its hierarchy is defined to include the lower numbered functions. This is more or less the way it was found to occur in reality. It was most clear-cut for Things and Data and only a rough approximation in the case of People.

4. The lettered functions are separate functions on the same level, separately defined. The empirical evidence did not support a hierarchical distinction.

5. The hyphenated functions, Taking Instructions-Helping, Operating-Controlling, and so on, are single functions.

6. The Things hierarchy consists of two intertwined scales: Handling, Manipulating, Precision working is a scale for tasks involving hands and hand tools; the remainder of the functions apply to tasks involving machines, equipment, vehicles.

4

done," thus resulting in a more sharply focused picture of a job-worker situation, the place where behavior and technology interact.

An analyst needs these reference points because embedded in the language of description are the analyst's perceptions of the difficulty/complexity levels of the work being performed. These perceptions may be based on what an incumbent or supervisor tells the analyst and/or what the analyst judges from personal experience. By consulting the scales, the analyst can determine the levels attached to the behaviors implicit in the language used to describe the job.

The Things, Data, and People functional scales define functional/behavioral levels that are, in effect, skill levels. The Worker Instructions scale defines the mix of levels of prescription and discretion the job requires. The Reasoning, Math, and Language scales define the general educational development levels required to do the work. Thus, a job analyst is provided with reference points to evaluate the language he or she uses to describe a job and to determine whether the complexity levels implicit in that language are the ones intended.

THE ROLE OF BENCHMARKS

Experience has shown that the definitions of scale levels, although helpful, are not enough of a guideline, the vagaries of language being what they are. Practitioners want *benchmarks*, which are simply examples from jobs that have been rated at various levels of the aforementioned scales. Actually, when raters do their work, they generate personal benchmarks to achieve consistency, drawing on their personal experience and memory. However, the rating process can be better served by having common benchmarks that all raters can refer to as needed. The benchmarks in this volume are intended to serve this need.

Benchmarks are more concrete than generalized definitions of levels, which border on the abstract. An example of both a generalized definition of a level from the FJA scale for Data—Analyzing—and two benchmarks that illustrate it demonstrates the difference and the value of both:

Analyzing: At this level, the individual examines and evaluates data (about things, data, or people) with reference to the criteria, standards, and/or requirements of a particular discipline, art, technique, or craft to determine interaction effects (consequences) and to consider alternatives.

Task 1: Review/evaluate resumes and/or applications received for a current job opening and prepare a summary report of qualifications of applicants, drawing on knowledge of job requirements and allowable equivalencies and relying on writing, analytical, and computer skills in order to determine which applicants meet the minimum requirements of the position and can be sent to the hiring supervisor for review.

Task 2: Consider/evaluate work instructions, site, and climatic conditions, nature of load, capacity of equipment, other crafts engaged in the vicinity, drawing on work order and experience and relying on analytical skill in order to situate (spot) crane to best advantage.

These two benchmark tasks not only manifest the worker action language for analyzing but also the knowledge, skill, and ability (KSA) supporting the behavior.

Benchmarks are tasks taken from FJA task banks. A *task bank*, an example of which can be found in Appendix C, is an inventory of the tasks that incumbents in a particular job have indicated they perform to turn out the outputs that they were hired to produce. The tasks are stated in the words of the incumbents.

Why tasks and not jobs for benchmarks? As is described in chapter 3, the simple reason is that jobs are much too vague an entity on which to hang an objective value. Tasks are much more stable units of work. In fact, quite a range of scale values can apply to the various tasks of a job.

ADDING BENCHMARKS

Ultimately, users will want to develop their own benchmarks using tasks drawn from job analyses and consensus ratings carried out in their own organization. Information on ordering a computer disk from the publisher is available at the end of the Preface of this book so that human resource specialists can more easily compare tasks from a variety of jobs in their organization with those included here. In this way the tasks will be constantly available for review and amendment if necessary. The authors hope this activity will inspire human resource specialists in these organizations to communicate with them. Constant updating of experience in using the benchmarks may thereby result in revision where necessary. Comparing the benchmarks against the level definitions of the scales may result in improvements of these definitions as well. As is evident, none of this material should be regarded as written in stone.

SUMMARY

Organizations, to achieve the essential objectives of fairness and equality in their human resource management activities, must do so on the basis of objective, reliable, and valid information about their job requirements. To obtain such information they carry out job analyses. The job analyses present serious problems mostly having to do with the language in which they are written. FJA is a method of job analysis that advocates the use of language in a specific and precise manner and makes use of scales as a referent framework within which to comprehend the job information collected. It is in this sense that the language of job description is controlled. Defining scale levels for functional skills, worker instructions, reasoning, math, and language has proven to be quite helpful. However, practitioners have expressed a need for benchmarks both to facilitate the use of the scales and to increase the reliability and validity of the data.

OUTLINE OF THIS BOOK

Chapter 2, "Background and Overview," provides a brief historical review of the 45-year history of FJA, as well as a contemporary context for the importance of job analysis. It also briefly describes current FJA practice in producing a job analysis database.

Chapter 3, "Communicating Job Information," discusses in detail the problems of communicating about work, including the subtle differences involved in the choice of words. It also explores the reason for focusing on tasks rather than jobs and the crucial role of level and orientation measures (Worker Function scales) in defining a task.

Chapter 4, "Enabling Factors: Scales of Worker Instructions and General Educational Development," provides a detailed description of the scales and their role in enabling behavior. These scales help define the KSAs involved in tasks. It also includes a discussion of the meaning of experience.

Chapter 5, "The Structure of an FJA Task Statement," describes how a standard English sentence is used as a framework for systematically incorporating all the essential information needed for human resource management including the enablers, knowledge, and instructions.

Chapter 6, "Writing Task Statements: Style Guidelines," explores the practical procedures and the pitfalls to be avoided when constructing task statements using FJA concepts.

Chapter 7, "Generating Benchmarks," describes the methods used to develop the benchmark tasks as reliable and valid indicators of scale values.

Chapter 8, "The Benchmark Tasks for the Seven Scales," also includes a list of jobs from which the benchmarks were selected: 49 task banks, 22 job definitions in the *Dictionary of Occupational Titles*, and selected tasks from the Upjohn Institute Task Bank. The appendices are as follows:

- Appendix A is a complete version of FJA scales with definitions of the levels.

- Appendix B is a chart comparing the Worker Function scales used herein with those in use in the U.S. and Canadian Occupational Classification Systems. A brief note is provided to explain the difference.
- Appendix C provides a sample list of tasks for a functional job analyst. It shows a product of an FJA workshop, namely, a task bank; it indicates the source of benchmark tasks; and it illustrates the range of ratings for each task and the interplay of function and KSAs in a job assignment.
- Appendix D is a presentation of Nature and Origins of Functional Job Analysis given at the 100th anniversary convention of the American Psychological Association.
- Appendix E is an application of FJA and the rating process to job evaluation demonstrating how every bit of information—including that of a few additional simple scales such as Strength and the Consequences of Error—converts to useful data for wage and salary administration.
- Appendix F is a bibliography. Although it includes sources referred to in the text, it is mainly a way of tracking the growth, development, and applications of FJA over the past 45 years. Critiques of FJA are included. It is not an exhaustive bibliography.

Chapter **2**

Background and Overview

This chapter provides a brief historical review of the 45-year history of FJA, as well as a contemporary context for the importance of job analysis. It also briefly describes current FJA practice in producing a job analysis database.

HISTORICAL NOTE FOR FJA

FJA is a major approach designed to achieve objective, reliable, and valid job descriptions. It was conceived in the late 1940s by Fine in response to the need for improvements in the *Dictionary of Occupational Titles*, the basic informational source book of the U.S. Employment Service, used to classify workers registering for unemployment insurance and applying for work. The existing second edition that had served so well to place civilians in military positions during World War II and then return soldiers to civilian life had manifested many flaws that cried out for correction. As a result, research was undertaken by the U.S. Department of Labor in the 1950s to achieve a sounder instrument. This research, known as the Functional Occupational Classification Project, resulted in the revision of the classification system and format of the *Dictionary*, starting in 1965. The results of the research were also adopted by the *Canadian Classification and Dictionary of Occupations*.

BACKGROUND FOR THE PRESENT MANUAL

The original publication of the FJA scales by the W. E. Upjohn Institute for Employment Research (Fine & Wiley, 1971)[1] contained some benchmark tasks drawn from extensive job analyses in the social services field, but only for the worker function scales. These job analyses had been sponsored by

---

[1]Fine, S. A., & Wiley, W. W. (1971). *An introduction to functional analysis*. Kalamazoo, MI: D.E. Upjohn Institute for Employment Research.

the Rehabilitation and Social Service Agency, a major division of the U.S. Department of Health, Education, and Welfare,[2] with the consultative assistance of the Upjohn Institute. The product of that work was a national task bank of about 1,100 tasks (ERIC), which served as a source for the benchmarks.

The publication of the revised scales (Fine, 1989)[3] did not include benchmarks. Its primary purpose was to provide users with an updated version of the scales. This publication was both a revision and an expansion of the 1971 document. Like the original manual, it focused on the problems associated with communicating job information and the means for dealing with those problems—a means embodied in the practice of FJA.[4] Six functional levels had been added to the Worker Function scales and some definitions adjusted accordingly.

THE PRACTICE OF FJA

During the 1970s and 1980s, interest in and use of FJA had increased considerably, stimulated, no doubt, by legal imperatives and as the result of training workshops given during this time.

Since the 1970s, Fine has conducted 3- to 5-day workshops for human resource management specialists to introduce them to the principles and procedures of Functional Job Analysis. More recently, for those interested in practicing the craft, this introduction has been followed by a two-stage procedure: (a) observation by a candidate of a certified analyst conducting an FJA focus group, and (b) a performance evaluation of the candidate conducting an FJA focus group by the certified analyst. Certification usually follows this process.

The focus group is the centerpiece of FJA technique, the primary data-gathering technology. Six subject-matter experts (SMEs), representing the range of expertise in a particular job in a work organization, are invited to participate as a group for 2 days in an off-the-job environment to describe the work they do and how they do it. The invitation indicates that they will be creating their own job description with the guidance of an FJA facilitator (analyst). The workshop itself centers around the SMEs' answers to five questions:

1. What do you get paid for (outputs)?
2. What knowledge do you need to produce the outputs?
3. What skills and abilities do you need to apply the knowledge?
4. What specifically do you do to accomplish each output (tasks)?
5. What performance standards, both those of management and your own, do you strive to achieve in your work?

---

[2]Now the U.S. Department of Health and Human Services.
[3]Fine, S. A. (1989). *Functional job analysis scales.* Milwaukee, WI: Sidney A. Fine Associates.
[4]A book on the theory and applications of FJA is now in preparation.

Their answers to these questions are noted on flip charts—large pads on easels from which pages can be torn off—and taped to the wall. They can go back to any page at any time to change what they will. The skill of the analyst includes achieving participation from all participants, organizing what they say into FJA format using their words, and obtaining their approval. Following a simple edit of the material they have produced, it is sent back to them for their final edit, approval, and sign off affirming that the task bank covers 95% of what they do.

THE NEED FOR JOB ANALYSIS

The current need for job analysis came up in the congressional hearings conducted in May 1993 in support of legislation that would develop national occupational skills standards and assessments. At those hearings, Paul Sackett, PhD and president of the Society for Industrial and Organizational Psychology, testifying on behalf of the American Psychological Association, stated that the legislation needs guarantees that the assessments will be technically valid and reliable. The bill being considered, he pointed out, did not adequately recognize the importance of job analysis. "If skill standards are the foundation of a high-performance work force, then job analysis is the cornerstone on which this initiative, and similar efforts, must rest," he said.

Sackett was contributing to the deliberations of the Goals 2000: Educate America Act, an education reform bill. In effect, he was saying that standards set for students must be fully cognizant of standards set for employment, and job analysis is the fundamental base for these standards. Such standards would contribute to the decisions made with regard to curricula and training materials and would be a link to the everyday decisions made in human resource management.

These decisions included determining:

- The worth of a job in relation to other jobs, usually on the basis of its relative difficulty and or complexity.
- The level and amount of training required by incumbents to reach normal production.
- The standards by which performance on the job is evaluated.
- The qualifications (KSA requirements) needed to select applicants.
- The design of jobs so that tasks contribute to a smooth work flow at a productive pace.

An additional powerful incentive for objective job analysis has been civil rights legislation (e.g., Civil Rights Act of 1964 and the Americans With Disabilities Act of 1992). This legislation seeks to forestall discrimination in employment by requiring a clear indication of the job relatedness of a variety of qualifications.

Whether educational standards, personnel operations, or civil rights legislation, the need exists for clear, concrete, definitive, dependable, insightful, and objective information.

OVERVIEW OF FJA BENCHMARKS AS A COMMON METRIC OF WORK PERFORMANCE

As indicated in chapter 1, FJA seeks to achieve quality information through language controls. The language controls contribute to both the vehicle for communicating work performance (the task statement), and the nature of work performance—the elements represented by the FJA scales that link worker requirements and worker qualifications (scale ratings). This conceptualization is represented in Fig. 2.1.

The model presented in Fig. 2.1 indicates the interdependence of the descriptive and analytical facets of FJA.

1. The analyst organizes task information collected from SMEs according to the English sentence model. This structured model ensures that the information collected is a clear, consistent, and reliable description of the work performed according to SME's experience.

2. While documenting the task information, the analyst mentally draws on the common metric for understanding work that is provided by the FJA Worker Functions scales and, to a somewhat lesser extent, the Worker

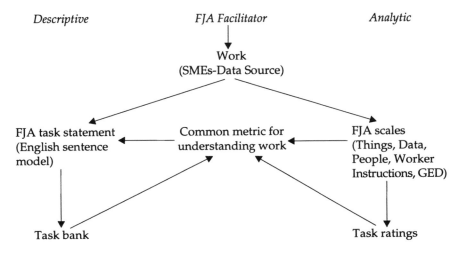

FIG. 2.1.   A conceptual model of the FJA process.

Instructions and General Education Development (GED) scales. This common metric guides the analyst in asking further questions, if necessary, to clarify the nature of the work and more precisely state the action(s) performed in each task.

3. The collected task statements that describe the work are assembled into a task bank.

4. The Task Bank, which documents the work performed in the job, can then be analyzed according to the FJA scales. The result of the analysis process are FJA scale ratings of each task, which provide a common metric for comparing all tasks.

Chapters 3 and 4 elaborate on the task ratings, whereas chapters 5 and 6 deal with the structure of the task statement. The back-and-forth aspect of the thought processes indicated here is dealt with in detail in chapter 6.

Chapter 3

Communicating Job Information

This chapter discusses the problems of communicating about work, including the subtleties involved in the choice of words. It also explores the reason for focusing on tasks, rather than on jobs and the crucial role of Level and Orientation measures in defining a *task*.

OVERCOMING THE DIFFERENT PERCEPTION OF COMMON TERMS

One of the questions asked of participants in an FJA training workshop is: "What do you do in your job?" For example, in a workshop conducted for personnel workers in the social welfare field that included some social workers, the question was: "What do social welfare workers do?"

In their answers, most participants made very similar statements. These statements included interviewing clients to determine their problems and counseling and guiding clients on problems of personal and social adjustment. When participants were questioned further as to what specifically they did when they interviewed or counseled clients, similarities tended to fade. Some said that when they interview and counsel they talk with the client to obtain certain kinds of information about him or her, giving pertinent information in return, following a standard format and established procedures.

Others said they give encouragement, advice, and suggestions to the client on a personal basis—much like a peer or family worker—on how to use community institutions or services appropriate to the client's situation. Still others said they serve as a source of technical information and help the client to define, clarify, or increase his or her understanding of stated problems and personal capacities for dealing with them. A few described what they do as working with the client on problems of overall life adjustment, following clinical, therapeutic, or professional principles.

Although the language used initially was almost identical, it soon became clear that words such as interview and counsel had quite different meanings for different workers. In most cases, the different meanings suggested differences in the nature and level of the skills and knowledge required of the workers. What appeared initially to be a common ground of understanding among participants quickly evaporated when they expanded on their understanding of the descriptive terms they commonly used. This was frustrating and confusing to participants. Especially troublesome was the apparent lack of any kind of framework within which the participants could reasonably discuss, understand, and, to some degree, resolve their differences and disagreements.

On a casual, conversational level, the various individuals could more or less agree on the work of social welfare workers, despite the fact that they may have come from different places in the organization, for example, selection, training, supervision, or classification. However, a problem developed when they had to agree on firm criteria defining the level of the job for training, performance appraisal, or job evaluation purposes. At this point, they drew on their different points of view and came up with disparate conclusions. Often, many of the participants lacked significant contact with workers in their actual positions that would allow them to test their assumptions about what workers were doing and what they needed to qualify. In effect, they were like the six blind men and the elephant, each touching the creature in a different place and feeling or reporting a different configuration. They were all correct. What was needed was a conceptualization of the situation that would provide the participants with a common reference point for their observations whereby they could achieve a common understanding.

Part of this conceptualization was the realization that the "job" was too fluid, too amorphous, too unstable, to focus on. It was not necessarily the same in any two organizations despite a core of things that might be the same. This core consisted of quite stable elements, namely, tasks. What was needed was a way of filtering the casual use of language in job descriptions so that the confusion could be seen for what it was—differing perceptions of the same basic "creature." What was also needed was a way of standardizing the formulation of tasks so that their stability could be firmly established.

This conceptualization now permitted a restatement of the problem of communicating about work, namely, that tasks needed to be understood as fundamental units of work, and that jobs were made up of a variety of tasks. Job titles were nothing more than broad, even casual indicators of an area of work. Recruitment, selection, training, supervision, and classification required focusing on tasks to carry out their missions and to fulfill their objectives.

THE "TASK" AS FUNDAMENTAL UNIT OF WORK

The definition of a *task* in the original edition of *Introduction to Functional Job Analysis* (Fine & Wiley, 1971)[5] has held up quite well.[6] It is as follows:

> A task is an action or action sequence, grouped through time, designed to contribute a specified end result to the accomplishment of an objective and for which functional levels and orientation can be reliably assigned. The task action or action sequence may be primarily *physical*, such as operating an electric typewriter; or primarily *mental* such as analyzing data; and/or primarily *interpersonal* such as consulting with another person. (pp. 9–10, emphasis in original)

The only changes made in this definition for the present volume are a matter of style. It now reads:

> A task is an action or action sequence, carried out over time, designed to contribute a specified end result to the accomplishment of an objective and for which functional levels and orientation can be reliably assigned. Functional level refers to level of difficulty of the action or action sequence and orientation to the extent the action or action sequence draws on *physical potential* as in operating an electric typewriter; *mental potential* as in analyzing data; and/or *interpersonal potential* as in consulting with another person.

"WHAT WORKERS DO": FUNCTIONAL LEVEL AND ORIENTATION DEFINED

What does "And for which functional levels and orientation can be reliably assigned" mean in the definition just given?

Functional level and orientation became the means for focusing on what workers do, the neglected part of job analysis, and the conceptual basis for developing a tool to control the language of job description and measure the complexity of tasks.

The following principles guided the development of this tool:

---

[5]Fine, S. A., &, Wiley, W. W. (1971). *An introduction to functional job analysis*. Kalamazoo, MI: Upjohn Institute for Emplyment Research.

[6]This definition grew out of and was consistent with a systems approach that was used to define the context in which tasks and work were performed. Briefly, the context described work-doing systems as consisting of three components: Worker, Work Organization, and Work. The master purpose of the work-doing system was to achieve Productivity, but along with it were the subsidiary purposes of Efficiency/Effectiveness and Worker Growth. Tasks were described as the fundamental unit of the work component (see Fine, S. A., & Wiley, W. W. [1969]. *A systems approach to new careers*. Kalamazoo, MI: Upjohn Institute for Emplyment Research.).

1. What workers do as they perform the tasks that make up their jobs, they do in relation to Things, Data, and People—the objects of their actions. All jobs involve the worker, to some extent, with machines, tools, equipment, and/or work aids (Things); with information or ideas (Data); and with customers, clients, or coworkers (People).

Workers function in unique ways in each of these areas. For example, when workers' tasks involve machines or equipment (Things), workers draw on their physical resources (strength, dexterity, motor coordination); when the tasks involve information and ideas, mental resources are brought into play (knowledge, thought, intuition, insight); when the tasks involve clients, customers, patients, interpersonal resources are employed (empathy, courtesy, warmth, openness, guile). Typically, workers are involved unevenly with these three primitives in any given task. The degree to which they are involved depends on the emphasis on the performance standards for one or another.

2. Although there may be an infinite number of ways of describing tasks in the context of their unique content and conditions, there is only a handful of significant patterns of behavior (functions) that describe how workers use themselves in relation to Things, Data, and People. Those patterns of behavior that can be articulated reliably have been defined in the Worker Function scales (see Fig. 1.1 and Appendix A), the primary tools of FJA. They provide a standardized, controlled vocabulary to describe what workers do in the entire universe of work.

For example, in using machines and equipment, workers *feed*, *tend*, *operate*, and *set up* machines or *drive/control* vehicles; or they *handle*, *manipulate*, or *precision-work* tools or portable power equipment.

In relation to information and ideas, a worker may *compare*, *compile*, *compute*, or *analyze* data.

In interacting with clients, customers, and co-workers, workers *serve*, *exchange information*, *coach*, or *consult* with people.

Although each of these worker functions is performed under widely varying conditions and involves a myriad of specific contents, each, within its scope and level of difficulty, calls for similar kinds and degrees of worker characteristics to achieve effective performance.

3. The functions in each of the three areas—Things, Data, and People—can be defined by a Worker Function scale (see Fig. 1.1) in which the performance requirements range from the simple to the complex in the manner of an ordinal scale. Because the scale is ordinal, the selection of a specific function to reflect the requirements of a particular task indicates that the task includes the lower functions and excludes the higher ones. For example, on scanning the Worker Function Scale for Data, when one selects the compiling function as the appropriate worker behavior to describe the way a worker must relate to information in a given task, two things are

decided: (a) the worker's performance is more complex than *copying* and less complex than *analyzing*; and (b) the worker must be able to perform all or at least comprehend all the data functions below *compiling*, but does not have to perform or comprehend higher functions, such as *analyzing* or *coordinating*.

4. The three hierarchies of Things, Data, and People functions provide two ways of systematically comparing and measuring the requirements of any task in any job. These two measures are *level* and *orientation*.

The *level* measure indicates the relative complexity or simplicity of a task when it is compared to other tasks. The level is expressed by selecting the function that best describes the pattern of behavior in which the worker engages to perform a given task effectively. The ordinal position of the function is the level measure.

The *orientation* measure provided by FJA indicates the relative involvement of the worker with Things, Data, and People in performing a task. A basic principle of FJA is that the worker is unevenly involved with the three primitives in any task. For example, in performing one task of a job, a worker may be involved almost exclusively with Data (e.g., 75%) for *compiling*; but to accomplish the task, the worker must also be involved interpersonally in *exchanging information* with co-workers (e.g., 15%), and with physical resources in *handling* various documents, paper, and pen (e.g., 10%). The lower percentages for the latter two functions indicate that they are not as demanding. The worker's total involvement with the task in question is, of course, 100%.

The *orientation* measure is expressed by assigning a percentage, in units of 5, to each of the three functions so the total adds to 100%. These percentages are estimates. The reliability sought is in the pattern of the three estimates, not in their absolute amount.

The orientation measure is a reflection of the performance requirements of a task, as noted earlier. In the example, the estimates assigned must be in accord with the independent judgment that this task will be evaluated overwhelmingly on its Data performance standards and quite lightly with regard to its People and Things performance standards. The training the worker must have to perform the task should emphasize and build on the mental skills required. The supervisor's instructions to the worker should emphasize and reflect the nature of the mental performance expected and the Data-oriented performance standards by which the worker's results will be judged.

RATING TASKS FOR FUNCTIONAL LEVEL AND ORIENTATION

The FJA analyst is trained to think in functional terms, that is, to translate the information obtained from SMEs in a focus group, or even when just hearing workers talk about what they do, into functional levels and orientation. Part of the discipline of getting specific information from incumbents is to gently press for specificity in what they do. Analysts know they have the information needed when they can mentally assign scale values with some assurance. In addition, when the task bank is completely edited and validated by the SMEs, the analyst may want to check the reliability and validity of each task (see Fig. 2.1). If they find they have trouble in making a rating they must rethink the information obtained and, if need be, return to the incumbents for clarification. It is desirable, if possible, to have a colleague independently rate the tasks for scale values, compare ratings, and arrive at a consensus.

The rating of the following task illustrates standing operating procedure (SOP):

> Ask client questions, listen to responses, and write answers on standard intake form, following an SOP with some leeway as to sequence of questions, drawing on knowledge of organization's procedure and relying on brief training in conducting a structured interview *in order to* record basic identifying information.

Simultaneous with receiving and organizing the information just given, the analyst judges this task as primarily a Data/People task, with emphasis on the former, and negligibly a Things task. In addition, the information is specific enough to satisfy the functional definitions for *copying* and *exchanging information*. The level and orientation for this task is then rated as:

Area	Functional Level	Orientation (%)
Things	Handling (1A)	10
Data	Copying (2)	50
People	Exchanging information (2)	40

Because the level and orientation measures can be applied to all tasks and to all jobs, the Worker Function scales provide a means for comparing all tasks and all jobs on a common basis. This is what was meant in the previous chapter by referring to FJA as a common metric. It should be anticipated that the ratings for the various tasks of a job can be quite varied. Jobs that have highly complex tasks can also have quite simple tasks as well. The question then is, "How can they be integrated to produce a single overall rating for a job?" The process is essentially a review process that notes and selects the highest ratings in the three functional areas. There might not be a single task that has the three highest ratings. It is necessary to emphasize that it is not an averaging process. The overall orientation rating would be a reconsideration of the relative emphasis to place on the Things, Data, and People standards for the entire job.

SUMMARY: FJA IS A MEANS FOR DEFINING/ANALYZING JOBS

FJA provides human resource specialists with a means to design viable jobs for their organizations from entry to professional levels. Applied to the jobs in the organization, FJA provides a base of accurate and comparable information of what workers do. Such information is essential for day-to-day personnel operations such as recruitment, selection, training, assignment, and supervision in order to maximize the use of the human resources in the organization. To develop such information, FJA provides the following two fundamental techniques:

1. A means for getting control of the language of description using the Worker Function scales and orientation estimates. The three hierarchies of worker functions, which define worker behavior from the simplest to the most complex levels, are a common language that makes it possible to reduce misunderstanding and inconsistency of interpretation among the many users of task information. In addition to controlling the language and meaning of what workers do, the Worker Function scales allow for comparison of what all workers do in terms of the level and orientation of their respective tasks on a common metric. This is a vital consideration in job evaluation and job design.

2. A means for getting to know the fundamental units of work in the organization, the tasks. The guidelines for writing task statements proposed in chapter 6 follow a specific form and structure and express what workers do to get work done. The task statements answer specific questions by expressing explicit worker actions and their expected results along with an indication of work aids, instructions, and sources of information. When written in this manner, objective information becomes available for generating performance standards and training needs.

Chapter 4

Enabling Factors: Scales of Worker Instructions and General Educational Development

This chapter provides a detailed description of the Worker Instructions, Reasoning, Math, and Language scales and their role in enabling worker behaviors (functions). These scales help define the knowledge, skill, and ability (KSAs) involved in tasks. It also includes a discussion of the meaning of experience.

KSAs: ENABLERS OF BEHAVIOR

Behaviors draw on KSAs, enablers of behavior. The full scope of a behavior is not clear until we know the KSAs it draws on. The KSAs include the nature of instruction (the balance between prescription and discretion) and the levels of reasoning, math, and language involved. (When the latter—reasoning, math, and language—are referred to collectively, GED is used.) The same behavior (e.g., "read/review") can involve some variation in the levels of instruction, reasoning, math, and language, depending on the content of the work. FJA provides scales for estimating the levels of instruction, reasoning, math, and language required to carry out the behavior that produces the end result. Each of the scales is discussed separately.

WORKER INSTRUCTIONS

All job assignments have instructions. They are infrequently mentioned as such in job descriptions. Instead, there is usually a statement concerning the degree of supervision from "close" to "general." There may also be a statement that employees need to "work independently," presumably meaning they need to instruct themselves.

This is unfortunate. Nearly all jobs have varying sources of instruction. Some of the instructions are built into the training and orientation workers receive for their assignments; some are issued periodically or intermittently by supervision; and in still others, workers formulate for themselves. Jaques (1956)[7] provided terminology to describe the nature of these instructions, namely, *prescription* and *discretion*. Prescription refers to that aspect of an instruction that is specified and involves definite limits and/or procedures. Discretion refers to the use of judgment and allowed leeway in following procedures, guidelines, and specifications. All jobs involve both. Even simple production jobs involve small amounts of discretion, if only to judge when to stop a process in an emergency. Even the highest level jobs, such as president or chief executive officer, involve some prescription such as defined limits to their authority and the need to obtain sanction from a board of directors for certain actions. The instructions for any job can have a range of prescription and description. In the task example used earlier, the worker behavior and results as well as the work aid (which defines the kind of information to be obtained) are prescribed:

> Ask client questions, listen to responses, and write answers on standard intake form, following SOP with some leeway as to sequence of questions, drawing on organization's procedures and training and relying on skill in conducting a structured interview *in order to* record basic identifying information.

However, the worker is expected to use his or her own judgment (discretion) in determining the order in which the questions may be asked. The task statement, nevertheless, clearly describes behavior that involves more prescription than discretion. A more controlled assessment of the prescription/discretion mix can be obtained by using the tool designed expressly for that purpose—the Scale of Worker Instructions.

SCALE OF WORKER INSTRUCTIONS

The Scale of Worker Instructions (see Appendix A) provides a measure of the proportions of prescription/discretion that occur in task performance. The scale is an ordinal scale similar in construction and use to the Worker Function scales. It has eight levels. The lower levels of the scale involve task instructions that have higher prescription in proportion to the amount of discretion a worker is expected to use, whereas the higher levels represent task instructions containing less prescription and proportionately more discretion.

---

[7]Jaques, E. (1956). *The measurement of responsibility*. Cambridge, MA: Harvard University Press.

In applying it to the example task, one would read the definitions in the scale of the various levels to find which one most accurately reflects the mix of prescription/discretion indicated in the task statement. Level 1 is too low and Level 3 is too high, whereas Level 2 seems to fit the task best. Therefore, the task statement should be assigned a Level 2 worker instruction. This information brings into sharper focus the functional level of the behavior involved in the task, namely, *handling, copying,* and *exchanging information.* This clarity should make it evident why explicitness in writing task statements includes information indicative of the level of instruction involved in the task.

Once prescriptive instructions are learned and understood, following them requires very little judgment by the worker. That part of instructions represents areas where the worker is not required or expected to use personal discretion; in fact, if indicated prescription is not followed, it is likely to be considered either negligence or insubordination. Following prescribed instructions consistently is usually occasion for reward. Discretion requires considerably more mental effort. When a worker exercises discretion, much more ability, skill, experience, and training must be drawn on and focused on the task at hand. Decisions in this situation are more complex and have important consequences for the end result. On the one hand, the continual exercise of good discretion calls for special acknowledgment and recognition. On the other hand, the exercise of poor or inadequate discretion usually calls for a change of assignment or dismissal. It is especially important to note that the exercise of discretion usually involves prescribing instructions for oneself.

Jaques (1956) maintained that a worker's sense of responsibility is based on the amount of discretion exercised in the tasks that make up an assignment or job. By varying the prescribed and discretionary balance of the tasks of a job, the job's level of responsibility can be changed. This has profound implications for career development and employee involvement because the leading edge of growth in one's career is having the opportunity to undertake tasks involving increased discretion and hence increased responsibility.

GENERAL EDUCATIONAL DEVELOPMENT

A problem cited frequently by personnel specialists is that of determining worker qualifications for jobs. How does one determine the education and experience required to perform the tasks that make up a job? This is all the more crucial today when the qualifications need to be shown as job related in order to satisfy civil rights legislation. In this section we discuss the education requirements. Experience is dealt with following a discussion of the GED scales.

Educational requirements are generally concerned with the basic skills of reading, writing, and arithmetic as well as common sense or reasoning. Commonly, such requirements were set in terms of years of schooling, such as high school graduation. The assumption represented by such a requirement was that anyone who had completed high school would have mastered the basic skills and, in addition, would have acquired the self-discipline associated with regular attendance, following instructions, and getting along with peers and superiors. However true this may have once been, it cannot be relied on today. Furthermore, such a requirement is often irrelevant and certainly not job related. Diploma and degree requirements tended to screen out capable and motivated applicants from minority and disadvantaged groups, hence, the need for a more accurate measure—an operational measure—of educational requirements. This is the purpose of the GED scales.

THE SCALES OF REASONING, MATH, AND LANGUAGE

The GED scales for Reasoning, Math, and Language are independent of years of schooling. They are scales of functional performance, whereby each level of each scale is stated in terms of on-the-job type of behaviors. A person may have actually acquired the ability for such functional behaviors in work activities or through self-learning. Thus, the questions asked of applicants hinge on "what have you done?" rather than on "how many years of schooling have you completed?" Similarly, when analyzing task requirements, the concern is with the specific basic skills required, as represented by the levels in the scales, rather than time spent in schooling.

The GED scales embrace only those aspects of education that contribute to a worker's reasoning development and acquisition of functional knowledge of language and mathematics. Because the levels of the scales are functionally defined, they have a constant meaning independent of school grade attainment that, as noted, can have a variable meaning. Although in FJA the scales are used to indicate a job's requirements, they may also be used to express an individual's level of achievement.

The Reasoning scale relates to concepts, problem-solving, making judgments, and carrying out instructions. The Math scale relates to arithmetic, algebraic, and geometric operations with numbers and associated symbols. The Language scale relates to understanding, reading, writing, and speaking the words, expressions, idioms, and ideas of a specific language. Like the Things, Data, People and Worker Instructions scales, they are ordinal hierarchies.

The scales are used in the same manner as the Worker Instructions scale, namely, by comparing what is described in a task with the appropriate levels in each scale and selecting the number of the level that fits best.

In the task we have been using as an example, the selection would be as follows:

- *Reasoning:* The task would seem to require common-sense reasoning, which involves Levels 1 to 3; the number of different things to consider are more than Level 1 and do not appear to involve as many as Level 3. Therefore the selection is Level 2.
- *Math:* There is very little indication of math involvement, which prompts a selection of Level 1.
- *Language:* The task involves a good use of language, particularly to adapt to anyone who might come in seeking social service help. The purpose of the leeway in asking questions is to be able to make such an adaptation. The benchmarks in the scale to which the task more or less corresponds is "copy written material . . ." and "conduct house-to-house surveys. . . ." It involves more language ability than speaking to service personnel, yet does not require as much language ability as the interviewing task in Level 4. Thus, Level 3 is selected.

To summarize, the FJA ratings for the example task suggest that its satisfactory performance requires the ability to follow instructions in which the inputs and outputs are specified, but in which the worker needs to be able to use some judgment in following SOP. The worker needs to have common sense in dealing with a few variables. No significant math ability is required, but language ability is necessary to conduct a formal interview guided by an intake form and to adapt to the language level of the clients.

EXPERIENCE

Few words in the employment vocabulary are more overused, misused, and misunderstood than *experience*. Sometimes experience is used in the sense that a worker has "been around" and is "wised up" to an environment. Sometimes it is used to suggest that an individual knows how to get things done by using informal channels. Still another meaning is that a person has spent many years at what he or she is doing (which does not necessarily mean the person is any the wiser).

On the basis of discussions with hundreds of experienced workers, we have arrived at the following definition:

Experience: Skill and or wisdom attained through observation and participation in a particular activity (Webster's Dictionary). To be experienced is to have a personal database consisting of: (a) the performance of assignments according to procedures in which trained, and (b) knowing that actual assignments/events typically present unique aspects that require the stretching and bending of rules/ procedures through the use of judgment to get work done. The database supplies the worker with clues for dealing with unique events that are not yet ready for generalizing into new rules.

This definition reflects certain realities: No two "experienced workers" in the same occupation are necessarily experienced in the same way, and experience is highly individualized. This is the fundamental reason why management never knows exactly what its workers are doing and how the work actually gets done.

In the next chapter we turn our attention from the use of scales to assign relative values to job information (analysis), to organizing the job information into the structure of a basic English sentence (holistic). The focus is more on description than on scale values.

Chapter 5

The Structure of an FJA Task Statement

This chapter describes how a standard English sentence is used as a framework for systematically integrating all the essential information needed for human resource management applications.

THE STRUCTURE OF A TASK STATEMENT

The structure of a task statement is represented in Fig. 5.1. The two most important components of the task statement are the behavior (action) and the result. They are not clear-cut or obvious. They are part of the flow of what a worker is doing.

Both mind and eye, as well as other senses, tend to focus on the result and take the behavior (action) that led to the result for granted. When we listen to a virtuoso violinist perform, we respond primarily to the execution/interpretation of a passage, rarely giving thought to the study and practice that went into that execution. Yet it is in that study and practice

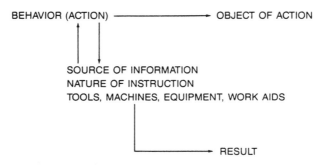

FIG. 5.1. The structure of a task statement.

that the knowledge, skill, and ability resides. The musician is likely to have abstracted passage after passage during study and practice in order to give the notes the appropriate emphasis for the effect he or she seeks to achieve.

Just as a passage in a musical composition can be selected for practice to achieve excellence in performance, similarly a task can be abstracted from the flow of work in a job assignment to comprehend the skills involved. Sometimes it is easy to separate the behavior from the result; sometimes it is quite complex, requiring considerable reflection. A major reason for this difficulty, in addition to the perceptual one, is that our language is very rich in the vocabulary of results and quite poor in the vocabulary of behaviors specific to work.

In Fig. 5.1, *the behavior* is the action the worker is expected to perform on, to, or with the object of behavior. The action can be represented by one predominant verb or several linked together as they might naturally occur in task performance as illustrated here:

Ask client questions, *listen* to responses, and *write* answers on standard intake form...

Prepare/write a course description...

Drive/control van...

The result is the outcome of the behavior (action) as enabled by the sources of information, the nature of the instruction, and the tools, machines, equipment, and work aids:

...IOT (in order to) *record basic identifying information.*

...IOT *inform field service personnel of course content, requirements and availability.*

...IOT *deliver children safely to a day care center.*

Although these two components enclose the task statement by defining what the worker does and what gets done, additional information is needed to help understand how the two are linked at the particular level represented by the choice of verbs for the behavior. This is the information represented by the enablers.

The enablers are the instructions and KSA elements that influence how the action/behavior is performed. They are the major source of information for the selection of level ratings from the Instructions and the Reasoning, Math, and Language scales described in the previous chapter.

- *Sources of Information* need to reflect the training, experience, and knowledge drawn on (which may be an area of scientific knowledge or specifications in a work order). This can be indicated generically (e.g., electronics) and then made more explicit within parentheses (e.g., basic theory including analog and digital, transistors, semi-conductors, silicon control rectifiers).

- *Nature of Instruction* needs to suggest the extent to which the worker is following a prescribed procedure and the extent to which discretion (judgment) is allowed. The more the task is discretionary, the more one can expect the choice of action verbs to reflect this. This cannot always be explicit as to level, but some information as to the specificity of the SOPs, or the guidelines, or the manuals, or the blueprints, or the schematics should be obtained. It should be expected that the incumbent SMEs are likely to be vague about this. Often they are using more judgment and experience than they care to admit or even know that they are using.

- *Tools, Machines, Equipment, Work Aids* are explicitly stated, naming them generically (e.g., test equipment) and explicitly in parentheses if several or many are involved (e.g., oscilloscope, meter, electronics tool kit).

The enablers link the behavior and result and help in understanding the choice of particular verbs selected to represent the behavior. A lofty result would need to have action verbs and moderators of equal status. This is an intangible that is hard to describe, but one immediately evident when not in sync. For example, action verbs used to describe the interview carried out to obtain identifying information (asks, listens, records) are quite different from those used to provide a technical explanation (consulting) of policy guidelines (queries, listens, explains, discusses). Along with the enabler information, this is one of the ways that internal validity becomes manifest in FJA.

HOW TO WRITE A TASK STATEMENT

The schematic shown at the beginning of this chapter is recast here with appropriate questions, the answers to which result in putting together the elements of a task statement. The questions are, in effect, a checklist of the information needed to serve a variety of personnel operations.

Who? (Subject).   The subject of a task statement is understood to be simply *worker*. The task statement does not in any way define what kind of a worker. As a result the task statement begins with the action or verb.

Performs What Action? (Action Verb).   A task statement requires a concrete, explicit *action verb*. Verbs which point to a process (such as *develop, prepare, interview, counsel, evaluate,* and *assess*) should be avoided. However, due to the shortage of explicit verbs to describe work behavior, there is a strong tendency to use them. At this point the analyst should ask: "What is actually going on? Is there more than one task involved?" If this questioning does not solve the problem, and using a broad verb still seems desirable, it should be accompanied by some qualifying verbs. In the example here, the analyst might have preferred to use *interview* in which case this verb would have been followed by verbs such as *query, listen, explain,* and *discuss* in the text of the task statement.

To Whom or on What? This refers to the Things, Data, or People objects of the actions. In the first example the objects are a Person (client) and Data (answers to questions). In the second example the object is Data (course description); in the third example it is a Thing (van).

Using What? A task statement should identify the tangible instruments, extensions of self, a worker uses to perform the task, such as Tools, Machines, Equipment, Work Aids. The self, which is, of course, the primary tool, is not mentioned because it is implicit in the subject. In the first two examples here the *tool* or extension of self is a writing instrument. If the instrument used is a stenotype machine or typewriter, it should be noted because that involves special skills. Since they are not mentioned, we can safely assume a pen and pencil, which, of course, are associated with writing skill. In the last example, the equipment is a van.

Drawing on What KSAs and Instructions? A task statement needs to identify in some way the nature of the instructions the worker follows and the sources of information. The phrase(s) relating to instructions should suggest what is prescribed and what is discretionary. This statement need not be in minute detail because some of this detail is initially obtained at the beginning of a FJA. However, it needs to be sufficient to illuminate the actions (verbs). We should be able to make a reliable judgment of the level on the Scale of Worker Instructions. Similarly, the sources of information noted should enable reliable judgments about the levels on the Reasoning, Math, and Language scales. For example:

> ...following standing operating procedure (SOP) with some leeway in the order with which questions are asked, drawing on organizational procedure and relying on brief training in conducting a structured interview....

> ...drawing on general background as instructor, the course materials and objectives, and relying on writing skill and ability to follow standard guidelines....

> ...drawing on knowledge of route and schedule, familiarity with the children, special considerations in driving young children and relying on ability to drive....

To Produce/Achieve What (Result)?   The purpose of the action performed must be explicit so that its relation to the objective is clear and, performance standards for the task can later be set. For example:

> ...in order to (IOT) record basic identifying information.

> ...IOT inform field service personnel of course content, requirements, and availability.

> ...IOT deliver children safely to school.

The standards will flow from the fact that the results part of the task statements must contribute to the organization objectives. (If it does not, then a reasonable question is: Why is it being performed?) In the first instance the objective is: To establish a client information system that enables workers to locate clients quickly and efficiently. In the second instance the objective is: To develop training programs that train field service engineers to fix equipment and keep customers happy. In the final instance the task result and the objective are identical.

COMPLETE FJA TASK STATEMENTS AND THEIR USEFULNESS

The complete FJA task statements will look like this:

> Ask client questions, listen to responses, write answers on a standard intake form following SOP with some leeway in the order in which questions are asked, drawing on organization's procedure training and relying on skill in conducting a structured interview IOT record basic identifying information.

> Prepare/write a course description following standard guidelines drawing on general background as an instructor, course materials, and objectives and relying on writing skill IOT inform field service personnel of course content, requirements, and availability.

> Drive-control a van drawing on knowledge of route and schedule, familiarity with the children, and special considerations in driving young children and relying on driving skill IOT deliver children safely to school.

A well-written task statement provides a clear and concise picture of the task. When it is written in this way, it becomes operationally useful, that is, it provides clear information that:

- Managers can use to assess the level of complexity of the task and compare its performance requirements with other tasks. They can also use it to determine whether the task is contributing to the objectives of the organizational unit.

- Supervisors can use to give clear, accurate instructions to workers and develop criteria for assessing whether the worker's performance is satisfactory.
- Selection personnel can use to specify worker qualifications (KSAs) needed to perform the task.
- Trainers can use to determine both classroom and on-the-job training for the worker assigned the task.

The next chapter essentially describes the experience of integrating the concepts of the previous three chapters in well-written task statements. In addition to rules, structure, and dynamics, some style guidelines are still necessary to achieve a degree of elegance in communicating task information.

Chapter 6

Writing Task Statements:
Style Guidelines

A written task statement records what a worker does, what is required to enable that action, and the result that occurs from such an action. The structure of a task statement, as presented in chapter 5, provides the conceptual framework needed to understand the nature of the work being performed and to capture it in writing. The purpose of this chapter is to describe how to write good task statements.

What appears simple in theory, however, is often not easy in practice. Writing clear and concise task statements requires effort. Poorly written tasks are often a confusing blur of work action and results, mingled with skills and knowledge. In contrast, a well-written task statement evokes a clear picture of what is going on in a job–worker situation. A good task statement reads smoothly and is neither too vague nor too detailed. The insights, explanations, comments, and tips that follow for writing effective task statements have grown out of the discussions among raters concerning the ambiguities and vaguenesses they encountered in rating benchmark tasks using the FJA scales. They are presented according to the three main components that comprise the FJA task statement model.

THE ACTION VERB

A concrete, specific, and explicit action verb at the beginning of a task statement is essential. A specific verb makes it easy to picture the work behavior being described. The action verb provides the primary focus for the task. Additional verbs describing additional behaviors may augment the primary verb if necessary. The following comments are directed toward beginning a task statement properly.

The active voice is used in task statements. We have adopted the convention of using verbs such as a supervisor or trainer might use to direct a worker or trainee. This avoids adding an "s" to the verbs and gives the task statement more directness and immediacy. (Verbs ending with an "s" are used in the function definition to suggest their generality).

> Remove laundry from washing machine...
> Write contracts for all departments...

Action verbs can be combined with a slash so that a specific action can be represented. This helps convey the specific meaning of the action. Up to three can be so combined, although combining only two verbs is much preferred. For example:

> Meet/confer with legislators...
> Monitor/coach youngsters placed under supervision...

The specificity of the verb used can often pose a problem when writing a task statement. In part, this is due to the limited domain of explicit verbs available with which to describe what workers do. This problem usually becomes evident when verbs that are identical to those listed in the Worker Function scales for Things, Data, or People are used. When this occurs, it indicates that a category of action is being referred to, rather than a specific action. For example:

> Coordinate efforts of rescue team...
> Schedule/plan rescue team activities...

The first verb in actuality refers to the class of worker behaviors identified in the Data Worker Function scale as Coordinating (Level 5B). A more specific form is presented in the second example. Schedule/plan would be a specific task that belongs to the Coordinating level of the Data Worker Function. The key distinction is that the first verb is more abstract and difficult to envision, whereas the second is more specific and easier to visualize.

It should be noted that it may not be possible to avoid the use of Worker Function level verbs in all situations. For example, the verb *set up* may be entirely appropriate for a task statement, with little in the way of alternative action verbs available to describe this behavior. The scarcity of good action verbs may necessitate the use of Worker Function terms in special cases. Whenever possible, however, the avoidance of Worker Function terms usually results in sharper task statements. When they are used they should be accompanied by descriptive data confirming their appropriateness.

The problem is also evident when verbs that refer to processes, rather than specific action, are used. Verbs such as *assess, fabricate,* or *develop* are examples of verbs that are more descriptive of a process than a specific action. There are generally two ways to handle this situation. The first is to replace the process verb with a specific verb that answers the question: "What is the worker doing when engaged in this process?" The second is to qualify or clarify the verb by combining with another verb. The following provide some typical examples:

Prepare an integrated report...versus
Prepare/write an integrated report...

Develop a teaching plan...versus
Develop/draft a teaching plan...

Some verbs are too vague to be useful as action verbs. *Complete, perform,* or *make,* for example, are not clear ways to begin a task statement. Replace with a more specific verb if possible, or ask yourself what the real action in the task statement is. This may require extra effort, but the clarity that is brought to the task statement is well worth it.

A common problem encountered in FJA is to confuse what a worker does with what gets done. It is relatively easy to start task statements with what is really the result of the task. There are a couple of ways this confusion can occur in a task statement. One way is to start a task statement with the term *provide*. The use of such a term is in essence presenting the results before the action by informing the reader of the task's purpose first. The following example illustrates a task statement that originally started with *provide* but was edited to capture the real action occurring in the task:

Provide volunteers with overview of agency services, informing them of policies, procedures, and funding sources, drawing on agency experience, and relying on interpersonal skills *in order to* have trained volunteers for agency operation.

Train/inform volunteers about agency policies, procedures, and funding sources, drawing on agency experience, and relying on interpersonal skills *in order to* provide volunteers with overview of agency resources and services.

The second example clearly portrays the primary action occurring in the task. Another hint that a task statement is confusing what a worker does with what gets done is when the word *by* followed by a verb is used in the task statement. The use of *by* usually indicates the key action in the task statement. The following example illustrates a task statement that was rewritten to focus on the primary action:

Respond to requests from state and county governments regarding the implementation of affirmative action *by accessing* applicant data records, compiling data specifics manually (e.g., race, gender, age, veteran status) using computer *in order to* meet the governmental report requirements.

Access applicant data records in computer, manually compiling data specifics relevant to requests from state and county governments regarding the implementation of affirmative action (e.g., race, gender, age, veteran status) *in order to* meet the governmental report requirements.

A task does not necessarily consist of only one action verb. However, stringing together several actions can sometimes resulting in a loss of focus and produce a job rather than a task description. As defined previously, "A task is an action or action sequence, grouped through time." An action sequence is represented in the task statement by using several action verbs to fully describe the task at hand. It is at this point that the skill and judgment of the analyst are especially challenged. The danger lies in attempting to capture a picture that has too much detail. This is illustrated in the following action sequence in a task statement:

Review/monitor the selection process, answer questions of hiring supervisor, advise on interviewing procedures, review documentation provided by supervisors in support of their recommendation for hire, and compare applicant to current staff in similar positions for equity in salary requested, drawing on knowledge of agency policies and procedures, relevant labor laws/regulations, internal managerial styles and preferences, and relying on verbal/written communication skills *in order to* ensure filling of vacancies with qualified applicants on a consistent basis.

As written, the task statement can be considered a first draft of what the analyst is trying to capture. The fact that there is too much here—although the actions strung together more or less go together—emerges when the analyst tries to rate the task. Although the task clearly involves "analyzing" and "consulting," it is very difficult to assign reliable orientation weights between Data and People. Too many performance standards come to mind. What becomes apparent is that practically a whole job is described. Here is a point where FJA can be especially helpful—namely, to reexamine the task from the standpoint of scope. It is possible that more than one task has been written. This is suggested particularly by the variety of performance standards that came up for consideration. With this in mind, two separate tasks, bringing the separate functions clearly into focus, are written as follows:

Review/monitor the selection process including documentation provided by supervisors in support of their recommendations for hire, drawing on agency policies and procedures, relevant labor laws/regulations, and relying on written communication skills *in order to* insure filling vacancies with qualified applicants on a consistent basis.

Advise hiring supervisors on interviewing procedures, answering their questions, drawing on agency policies and procedures, relevant labor laws/regulations and internal management styles and preferences and relying on verbal and interpersonal skills *in order to* support the supervisors in their recruiting of qualified applicants.

The advantage of this latter approach is that it separates the behaviors requiring data skills from those that focus on people skills. This can be especially useful in both job and curriculum design.

A couple of points are worth noting concerning the use of more than one action verb in a task statement. The first concerns writing task statements that focus on action sequences as in time and motion analysis. Such tasks can often sound like rigid mechanical procedures, with little apparent discretion on the part of the worker. SMEs sometimes unknowingly contribute to this formulation because it is relatively easy for them to relate their work in terms of sequences or procedures. Where possible, task statements that have such a microfocus on elemental action steps should be avoided. An exception might be the physical action sequences frequently associated with the operation of some machines, equipment, or vehicles.

The second point is mostly a matter of writing style. It is suggested that the follow-on actions in a task statement avoid the repetitive use of verbs with an "-ing" ending. The overuse of such verbs can be tedious and induce a ringing in the readers mind. Occasional use of verbs ending in "-ing" can help the flow of the task statement.

ADDITIONAL CLUES IN SELECTING ACTION VERBS

In general, some actions should be considered to involve repetitions and reactions without explicit statement (e.g., start/restart, align/realign, calculate/recalculate, call/recall, visit/revisit). However, in instances stating converse of the action (e.g., load/unload), it seems best to be explicit as it more fully describes the action.

Verbs that also serve as adjectives present special problems. In FJA, distinguishing between action, performance standard, and result is important, thus the indiscriminate use of such verbs is confusing (e.g., "clean"). We therefore suggest that such words be consistently used in one sense or another in a task statement.

The action sequences and procedures in jobs relating primarily to the processing of Things are very similar. This applies particularly to machine operations. Variety enters into Thing-oriented jobs when workers become involved with multiple materials and functions (e.g., planning, inspection, quality control).

ACTION ENABLERS

The middle of an FJA task statement describes how an action is enabled so the result can be achieved. Action can involve the use of specific equipment, require particular instructions, draw on certain knowledge domains, and/or rely on distinct skills and abilities in order for the result to be accomplished. Although there may be a wide variety of enablers that might be applicable to a task, only those that are primary to the achievement of the results should be included in the task statement.

The middle component can be thought of as having three subsections. The first section documents those factors external to the worker, such as equipment and instructions, which are required in the performance of a task. This section is introduced after the initial action phrase by terms such as *using*...or *referring to*...The second section details the knowledge required to perform the task and is introduced by the phrase *drawing on*....The last section describes the skills and abilities required to perform the task and is introduced by the phrase *relying on*....An examination of any of the task statements provided as benchmarks in this document reveals this skeletal structure.

Sometimes this structure is implicit rather than explicit. In tasks at the lowest levels of difficulty or complexity, the knowledge and skills are represented largely by the instruction and by the obvious use to which certain tools and equipment could be put. Similarly, tasks of a high worker function level may focus on KSAs with little, if any, work aids required. Nevertheless, the sections described serve as a conceptual outline that aids in the construction of a comprehensive task statement.

This approach to the presentation of the benchmarks is consistent with the manner in which the information was obtained from the SMEs. The reader will recall that the information for the middle component was elicited systematically in two ways. The first way followed the indication of outputs at the start of an FJA workshop. The SMEs were asked "What knowledge do you need to produce the outputs?" and then "What skills and abilities do you need to apply the knowledge?" These were separately listed and posted as a constant reminder and reference for comprehending the underlying resources involved in the tasks.

The second way was to obtain the task information from the SMEs according to the conceptual outline of a task statement. This conceptual outline is used in an accommodating manner rather than imposed as a rigid, mechanical procedure. The SMEs are guided initially to provide the action and whatever tools, machines, and/or equipment used to affect the action. Then the analyst will write on the flip chart *drawing on* to indicate the place for the primary knowledge, instruction, and education or training specifically relevant to the action. Following this, the analyst will write down *relying on* to indicate the place for primary skills, abilities, and experience essential for applying the knowledge and/or carrying out the task. Finally, toward the bottom of the flip chart, the analyst, will make a place for the result.

Typically, the three sections concerning the action enablers prove most useful for the more difficult and complex tasks. The effective description of more complex action requires the clear communication of how action enablers are involved. The skills and abilities required in tasks associated with lower levels of the worker functions, in contrast, are usually obvious and need not be overstated (e.g., requires literacy, common sense). Just as the composition of a picture requires focal elements, so too does the creation of a task statement require the proper use of action enablers. To include too many action enablers is to overpaint a picture of the task action. The write-up of the benchmark tasks, therefore, attempts to follow this concept, portraying action enablers appropriate to the task.

The diversity of information that could be included in the middle component of a task statement prevents a complete and comprehensive discussion. Instead, some general comments are provided to assist in writing this portion of the task statement:

- Be specific. The phrases and terms should be as precise as possible so the meaning is clear. For example, *communication skills* is a bit broad when *persuasion skills* is meant in a sales-oriented task statement.

- Focus on the important action enablers, the ones likely to be involved in the performance standards of the task. A tendency to include KSAs for the sake of completeness rather than for how important they are to the performance of the task can easily occur. Focusing primarily on the importance of action enablers, rather than on their relevance, helps keep task statements shorter, more readable, and easier to rate on FJA scales.

- Use consistent terms and structure. The phrases *using...*, *drawing on...*, and *relying on...*provide consistent terms within a natural structure that contribute to the overall quality of task statements. The use of alternative terms such as *utilizing* instead of *using*, and *based on* instead of *drawing on* are a bit more ambiguous, and should be avoided. Similarly, the three sections outlined here seem to work best in that order. That is, the tangibles required to perform an action, aided by a knowledge base, and facilitated by skills and abilities seem to form a natural progression from action to result.

THE RESULTS OF AN ACTION

The last component of a task statement describes the results of an action, the purpose or objective for which an action is engaged. This component is always

introduced by the underlined phrase *in order to* (IOT). Writing the results of
a task statement is relatively easy, given the natural bias people have to think
about work more in terms of what gets done rather than what one does. A few
comments, however, concerning the results section should be noted.

The results of the task should correspond to the primary orientation of
the action. More specifically, the results of an action should mirror the
orientation of the action toward Things, Data, or People functions. A task
highly oriented toward People, for example, should not have a result that
is highly Things-oriented. The more the main action and results agree in
Worker Function orientation, the easier the task is to understand.

The results should be closely and clearly related to the action. The more
distant the result is from the action, the less understandable the task
becomes because the relation between the action and the result requires
additional inference. Results distal to the action can also blur the conceptual
boundary between results and organizational objectives. The results of
several tasks are usually required to achieve an organizational objective. In
fact, one way for an organization to review its operations is to check if the
results of task actions associated with an output cumulate in an
organizational objective. In the following example, the first phrase in the
results section is proximal to the action in the task, whereas the second
phrase is more distal and related to general organizational objectives.
Additional tasks are required to achieve the more distal part of the result.
Removing the second phrase in the results portion of the task statement
here creates a sharper task:

> Counsel/advise clients having personal problems, drawing on knowledge of
> counseling methods, theory and guidelines, and relying on interpersonal and
> communication skills and ability to establish rapport *in order to* help client gain
> insight into personal problems, and improve the quality of community living.

Alternative phrases or words may imply an IOT relation when not intended
or needed. Phrases such as *so as, so as to, to,* and *in order that* are synonyms
for IOT, and should be avoided. The use of such terms within the body of
the task statement is essentially redundant with the use of IOT, and makes
the task less understandable. As a point of style it should be mentioned that
no comma is needed before IOT because it is implied by the phrase.

ADDITIONAL COMMENTS

A few additional suggestions are provided here to assist in writing clear,
concise, and complete task statements.

Adverbs and adjectives imply performance standards and should be
avoided whenever possible. The use of adverbs and adjectives in a task
statement shifts the focus away from describing the tasks to that of the

proficiency or standards required in task performance or task results. This tendency can most easily occur in the results component of the task statement. The first example below illustrates a task that implies several performance standards, whereas the second task is an edited version of the first:

> Train/instruct program personnel in the *proper* use of a computer, using *relevant* hands-on demonstration, drawing on personal knowledge and experience with the computer system, and relying on *well-developed* instructional skills *in order to* enable program personnel to *independently* maintain financial records.

> Train/instruct program personnel in the use of a computer, using hands-on demonstration, drawing on personal knowledge and experience with the computer system, and relying on instructional skills *in order to* enable program personnel to maintain financial records.

Use parentheses sparingly. They are helpful when used to amplify an unfamiliar term, for example, *running board* (the day's instructions) for bus operators, or to illuminate a general term, for example, *respond to messages* (electronic mail, fax, telephone), or to clarify jargon, for example, *FMIs* (field modification instructions). However, the overuse of parentheses can be an irritant to the smooth reading of a task statement. Although the use of parentheses is a matter of individual judgment, each use should be carefully scrutinized. They should be avoided if they distract more than they inform, or if the task can be rewritten to avoid them. The terms *such as* or *including* can often be used in place of parentheses.

The degree of discretion a worker has in performing a task is reflected in the language used in a task statement. The phrases, *as appropriate, as necessary*, and *as required* can reflect a degree or range of discretion, depending on the context in which they are used.

Writing effective task statements is a skill, and like all skills it is developed with practice. Although it is recognized that task statements can get rather long and appear unwieldy at times, there is nevertheless an elegant quality that is radiated from a well written task statement. An effective task statement portrays in words a sharply focused picture of work action.

When task statements are prepared in the manner described here, according to FJA procedures and with the FJA scales in mind, it is then possible to use the information with confidence for such human resource applications as job evaluation as shown in Appendix E. The same information can also be used effectively for job design, developing performance standards, and designing training curricula, applications dealt with in detail in the forthcoming book mentioned earlier.

Chapter 7

Generating Benchmarks

THE BENCHMARKING PROCESS

The process of developing benchmarks for FJA scales consisted of two major stages: (a) the rating of task statements from a wide variety of task banks on all FJA scales, and (b) the selection of task statements rated in Stage 1 to serve as illustrative task statements for each of the FJA scale levels. The entire benchmarking process emphasized consensus, in both ratings made and tasks selected. The use of consensus ensured a common understanding of the FJA scales and task statements developed, and that the benchmarks ultimately selected were thoroughly understood and considered. It is this common understanding of the task statements, and their relation to each of the FJA scales, that underlies the benchmarks for FJA scales.

Rating FJA Task Statements to Serve as Benchmarks

Graduate students in industrial/organizational psychology who had previously attended a 3-day workshop in the theory and practice of FJA served as the raters on the FJA benchmark project. As part of the FJA workshop, raters had participated in task rating exercises with the Things, Data, or People function scales. Before rating task statements for the FJA benchmark project, the trained raters engaged in an additional task-rating exercise to become familiar with all the FJA scales and to have the opportunity to address any possible ambiguities or concerns in their use.

FJA task banks from more than 40 jobs, mostly from the social services area, were reviewed by the trained raters, resulting in the consensus rating of more than 650 task statements. Pairs of trained raters were assigned to each task bank. Each rater individually rated each task statement of a task bank on all the FJA scales. Raters were encouraged to limit rating activity to 2 hours or less to maintain interest and alertness in the rating process.

The raters then met to discuss their task ratings and to reach a consensus rating for each task statement.

Attaining Consensus Among Raters

The consensus process for achieving reliable and consistent ratings was explicit. In no case were raters allowed to average ratings to achieve consensus. When there was a difference between raters in a task rating (in the majority of cases, initial ratings were within one level of each other), each rater was to describe the phrasing and data in the task statement that led him or her to make the particular rating. In addition, raters were encouraged to refer to the scale-level definitions to anchor their ratings. In the overwhelming majority of cases, the differences in ratings were resolved by simply listening to each other's rationale. The differential appropriateness of their task ratings quickly emerged in discussions between raters and in this manner raters often readily reached consensus.

When differences in ratings could not be resolved by the process just discussed, the raters were required to examine what changes in the wording of the task statement were required to achieve consensus. Such a change in wording would usually reflect a salient feature of the scale definition that had been selected. In some instances, the point of view of a third rater was requested and reflected on before a final rating was made. At no time was a final rating arrived at by pressure of authority or by majority vote.

Selecting FJA Benchmarks

Once a large selection of task statements had been rated, raters were asked to select examples of task statements that they thought best conveyed the definition and nature of each level of the FJA scales. Three raters met to review and nominate task statements to serve as illustrative benchmarks. No rankings or other quantitative method was used for selecting the final benchmarks used in the benchmark reference guide. Rather, only those task statements that the raters agreed best conveyed the definition and intent of each scale level were selected. When possible, benchmarks were chosen to provide a range of illustrative tasks to represent a scale definition. In addition, benchmarks for the Things, Data, and People function scales were chosen whenever possible to represent tasks wherein the orientation to the particular scale and level was considered high (65%-90%), medium (35%-60%), or low (5%-30%) based on the performance standards that were salient.

The goal of the task nomination process was to have between 5 and 10 task statements for each level of each FJA scale. In most cases, there were many task statements to choose from. For some scale levels, however, the variety of task statements available was limited. In some cases, this was due to some FJA scale levels not occurring widely in many jobs. For example, the new People scale level *Leading* has not been used extensively, nor does it seem to be a function widely represented, and examples of this scale level are therefore hard to acquire. In other cases, the scale level simply did not occur often in the sample of jobs rated.

The usefulness of the FJA benchmark reference guide is determined to a great extent by how well illustrated each scale level is. To augment those scale levels that had fewer than five benchmarks, specific task statements were selected from a sample of jobs that appeared to represent those desired characteristics. These individual task statements were then submitted to the rating process previously described. For example, selected task statements from several high-level professional jobs were rated, and task statements that were applicable to scales not yet adequately illustrated were considered for nomination. Through this process many of the more difficult to find benchmarks were included in the process.

The final assembly of the benchmarks for FJA scales was made by both authors. When making the final review, some tasks were judged to be a poor fit with the body of tasks selected for a particular level. Because the original raters had dispersed by this time, these tasks were either discarded (a handful of tasks) or moved. Moving tasks was a consensus judgment of the authors; the movement was always to an adjacent level, up or down.

For a few scales, there was still an inadequate sample of benchmark tasks. Likely job definition sources in the *Dictionary of Occupational Titles* were resorted to and tasks formulated from them that met the criteria of the definitional level of the scale. In this instance, the authors were essentially acting like users of this document, in effect matching task data to scale definitions and available benchmarks.

THE FJA BENCHMARKS: THE FINAL PRODUCT

Although there were more than 650 tasks to choose from, not all task statements had the necessary qualities to serve as good benchmarks for FJA scale-level definitions. Conversely, there were numerous times that a good example for one scale might be a good example for several FJA scales. Of the more than 450 task statements that served as the benchmarks in the finished FJA reference guide, approximately 100 were used twice, with one of these uses occurring in either a Things, Data, or People function scale. This was considered an acceptable tradeoff to the insight gained from using a task statement twice.

The consensus process used does not mean that all benchmarks are of equal quality. The task statements used as benchmarks were written by various job analysts, all of whom have their own styles when it comes to writing task statements. The major difference, aside from the natural variance in the use of words, is in the amount of detail. The use of task statements selected from a variety of jobs, and written in different styles, however, helps illustrate the concept underlying the definition of each scale level. To some extent the style differences have been neutralized by editing the tasks to conform to the basic structure of task statements.

Using the FJA Benchmarks

The final product of this comprehensive process is found in the indexed section for each FJA scale. The user can easily flip to the FJA scale desired and consult the level that is felt to be appropriate for the task statement under consideration. The definition of each scale level is provided on the left-hand page, along with additional comments and helpful hints, where applicable, for effectively using that particular scale level. The page on the right contains the selected benchmark task statements that illustrate each scale-level definition. For some scale-level definitions there are several associated illustrative tasks, requiring the use of more than one page of example tasks. Users can consult the example tasks given to see if the task being rated is similar in nature to the examples provided. Users should not be surprised to find their tasks similar to those under consideration because the language available to describe worker behavior, as represented by the action verb in a task statement, is extremely limited.

The authors' practice in arriving at a decison about the scale level of a particular task is to verify the decision, once it is made, by comparing it with the tasks in the scale level below and above the level decided on. This is good practice in using ordinal scales because, as pointed out earlier, scale levels blend into one another.

Adding Local Data

This document and the available computer disk are designed to be user-friendly and cumulatively useful. Users are encouraged to append comments and considerations related to their use of the definition of scale levels directly in the book. They can also add their comments and task examples to the information on the computer disk. This will, of course, make the benchmarks more particular to their experience and more relevant to their needs. Over time, they will be able to track their ratings for consistency and have available documentation of their thinking relative to the rating process. It is the authors' hope that users will communicate their experiences, including questions, concerns, and practical decisions, so we can improve the benchmark information in future editions of this document.

Chapter 8 contains the selected benchmarks for each of the scales in the following order: Things, Data, People, Worker Instructions, Reasoning, Math, Language. Each of the scales has a brief introduction. The scale-level definition precedes the benchmarks for that definition. Wherever the authors' accumulated experience in formulating and rating tasks was thought to be helpful, that information is associated with the level definition as Comments and Helpful Hints. Where none appears it simply means that the scales and the rating procedure were sufficient to make reliable ratings.

Chapter **8**

The Benchmark Tasks for the Seven Scales

TASK DEFINITION SOURCES FOR BENCHMARK TASKS BY CODE AND TITLE

ARP	Academic Research Psychologist
ACT	Accountant
APS	Accounts Payable Specialist/Technician
ANI	Antenna Installer
ADD	Auto Design Detailer
BHO	Backhoe Operator
BUO	Bulldozer Operator
CTD	Center Director
CAT	Chief Accountant
CPM	Clothes Pin Machine Operator
CRS	Community Relations Specialist
CTR	Controller
COP	Counseling Psychologist
CRO	Crane Operator
DBA	Database Administrator
EXD	Executive Director
EXM	Executive Manager
FAM	Family Advocate
FCA	Food Counter Attendant, Meat Market
FRM	Framemaker
GED	GED Teacher
GRA	Grader Operator
GRM	Grinding Machine Operator
HSA	Head Start Administrator
HSN	Head Start Nutritionist

HST	Head Start Teacher/Assistant
HSV	Head Start Van Driver
HOT	Home Security Technician
HFC	Human Factors Specialist—Consumer Products
HFI	Human Factors Specialist—Information Display
ILL	Illustrator
IOP	Industrial/Organizational Psychologist
IRS	Information and Referral Specialist
INW	Insulation Worker
JAN	Janitor
JNP	Janitor, Nuclear Plant
LYR	Lawyer
LAT	Lathe Operator, Metal
MAT	Mathematical Technician
MIN	Minister/Clergyman
MMO	Manufacturing Machine Operator
NUR	Nurse
PSS	Payroll Supervisor Specialist
PSU	Personnel Supervisor
PHT	Physical Therapist
PIP	Pipefitter
PSC	Planning Supervisor—Commodities
PSR	Policy Service Representative
PPR	Power Press Operator
PRA	Program Analyst
PIS	Public Information Specialist
PPO	Punch Press Operator
PUA	Purchasing Agent
SHM	Shaping Machine Tender
SID	Siding Installer
SFM	Slip Form Machine Operator
SWF	Social Worker/Family Specialist
STW	Street Worker
SAC	Supervisor—AODA Counselling
SUR	Surveyor Assistant
SWB	Switchboard, Office Supply, Mail and Files Personnel
SYA	Systems Administrator
TLD	Team Leader
TRS	Training Specialist
TBE	Benchmarks in 1971 edition of Scales

THINGS FUNCTIONS SCALE

Working with Things literally means the physical interaction with tangibles, including taken-for-granted items such as desktop equipment (pencils, paper clips, telephone, handstamps, etc.). blackboards and chalk, and cars. Physical involvement with tangibles such as desktop equipment, and so on, may not seem very important in tasks primarily concerned with Data or People, but their importance is quickly apparent when handicap or ineptness occurs. An involvement with Things can be manifested in requirements for neatness, arrangements, and/or security of the workplace. Workers who make decisions or take actions concerning the disposition of Things (tools, materials, or machines) are considered to be working mainly with Data, although they physically handle Things (e.g., records, telephone, and catalogs).

The Things Functions scale includes: physical interaction with and response to tangibles—touched, felt, observed, and related to in space; images visualized spatially.

The arabic number assigned to definitions represents the successive levels of this ordinal scale. The A, B, C, and D definitions are variations on the same level.

Things Benchmarks

Level 1A: Handling

Definition.   Works (cuts, shapes, assembles, etc.) digs, moves, or carries objects or materials where objects, materials, tools, and so on, are one or few in number and are the primary involvement of the worker. Precision requirements are relatively gross. Includes the use of dollies, handtrucks, and the like; writing tools, telephones, and other desktop equipment; and the casual or optional use of tools and other tangibles.

Comments.   This is the basic tool-using function. This function is an obvious one for simple tool-handling tasks. In addition, it will frequently be used for tasks that are predominately Data- and People-oriented and have no significant involvement with tools or where tools (e.g., pencils, telephones, staplers, erasers) are incidentally and casually used and for which performance standards are not paramount. It is rated because the physical involvement is nevertheless there as part of the total involvement of the worker in the work getting done.

Please note that for low functional levels of the Things scale explicit reference to knowledge and skills is not always made as they can be readily inferred from the tasks. Explicit statement of knowledge and skills in this instance would be more of a hindrance than an aid to understanding the work performed.

Helpful Hints.   First, the words *clean* and *polish* are difficult in verb form because they can embrace several meanings; for example, action verbs, performance standards, and results. Because in FJA distinguishing between action (behavior), performance standard, and result is important for clarity, the indiscriminate use of such words can be confusing. Therefore, we propose that these words be used in one sense or another consistently in a task statement.

Second, when using verbs that are closely associated or identical with tools used, it is redundant to refer to them explicitly. For example, it is not necessary to specify "using a mop" when the action is "mops floor."

Level 1A: Illustrative Tasks

High (65%–90%).   Mop floor, immersing mop into bucket of polishing solution, removing excess with bucket squeegie, and using side to side overlapping strokes over entire floor, repeating the process after the floor has dried, following SOP *in order to* polish the floor. (JAN)

Medium (35%–60%).   Pick up newspapers at newsstand and mail at U.S. Postal Station in building, carry or drag (if very heavy) to mailroom, relying on physical strength and following SOP *in order to* have mail available for sorting and papers ready for delivery to persons designated. (SWB)

Seal funds of Crisis Center clients in an envelope while they are in the Crisis Center, place it in a locked box in a locked file, following SOP *in order to* provide safe-keeping service for client's money and food stamps. (FAM)

Low (5%–30%).   Train selected volunteers and/or work placements one-on-one on the job, informing them of funding sources, documented policies, practices, and procedures; demonstrating phone system operation and telephone etiquette; and showing how to use resource files and complete forms, drawing on experience and knowledge of the project and relying on interpersonal skill *in order to* break in the new people and provide them with the information needed to perform their job. (IRS)

(See page 72 for additional Handling tasks)

Things Level 1B: Feeding-Offbearing

Definition.   Inserts, throws, dumps, or places materials into, or removes them from, machines, equipment, or measuring devices that are automatic or tended/operated by other workers. Precision requirements are built in, largely out of control of worker.

Comments.   This is the simplest of the machine functions and is often an entry job to more involved machine functions. As technology has become computerized, this function has been integrated with more complicated functions.

Minor levels of feeding-offbearing are included in higher machine functions such as tending, operating, and setting up. Therefore, there are no examples of medium- or low-orientation feeding-offbearing tasks.

Helpful Hints.   The distinctions between Handling and Feeding-Offbearing can occasionally be quite marginal—both involve relatively simple handling. In the case of Handling, tools are usually used to process materials. In the case of Feeding-Offbearing, materials are typically fed into machines. There will be borderline situations.

Level 1B: Illustrative Tasks

High (65%–90%). Remove hospital laundry from dryer at end of drying cycle and place in laundry bag, following SOP *in order to* ready laundry for pressing room pickup. (TBE)

Load/place paper into feeding rack of duplicating machine, drawing on awareness of safety guidelines, following SOP *in order to* prepare machine for operation. (TBE)

Load/place dirty dishes, pots, pans, and other cooking and eating utensils into automatic dishwasher, following SOP *in order to* prepare machine for wash cycle. (TBE)

Place meat or fish on electronic weigh scale, drawing on knowledge of health guidelines for the handling of food, following SOP *in order to* weigh product and obtain weight/price label. (FCA)

Feed wooden clothespin blanks into machine that picks up, saws, and flares end of block, removing defective stock as necessary, drawing on knowledge of safe work procedures and following SOP *in order to* make parts for clothespins. (CPM)

Medium (35%–60%).

Low (5%–30%).

Things Level 2A: Machine Tending I—Material Products and Processing

Definition.   Starts, stops, and monitors the functioning of machines and equipment set up by other workers where the precision of output depends on keeping one to several controls in adjustment in response to automatic signals according to specifications. Includes all machine situations where there is no significant setup or change of setup, where cycles are very short, alternatives to nonstandard performance are few, and adjustments are highly prescribed.

Helpful Hints.   There are few synonyms for Tending. The analyst needs to expect, in many instances, to use *tend* as the operative verb in describing what the worker does.

Level 2A: Illustrative Tasks

High (65%–90%).   Check condensate pump and water glass on water column several times daily, listen for unusual noise indicating a problem, drawing on knowledge of and experience with boiler system *in order to* ensure boiler is operating properly. (JAN)

Remove/unlock part of stamp machine when the setting for specified amounts of money is low, bringing part to Post Office for resetting and returning it to machine *in order to* have adequate stamping resources. (SWB)

Remove laundry from washing machines at end of cycle for placement in dryer, remove accumulated lint from collecting screen in dryer, set time and temperature appropriate to laundry being dried, following SOP *in order to* dry laundry. (JNP)

Check boiler water level daily, adding water if low according to specifications *in order to* insure boiler is operating properly. (JAN)

Medium (35%–60%).   Tape interview, adjust tone and volume controls as necessary, stop recording, and label tapes at completion of session *in order to* record client interview. (TBE)

Low (5%–30%).

Things Level 2B: Machine Tending II—Data Processing and Duplication

Definition.   Starts, stops, and monitors the functioning of machines and equipment that are preprogramed to perform the basic functions involved in data processing, document copying, and printing. Machines/equipment are activated at keyboard terminals or touch-control panels and can accomplish special effects for particular activities through the input of special codes. Nonproductive use of calculators, typewriters, and similar office equipment is included here.

Helpful Hints.   Sometimes a borderline decision relative to two adjacent functions is influenced by the amount of judgment involved in the task. Tasks that require more involved judgment will tip the decision in favor of a higher level function. This will also be reflected in the Instructions rating of the tasks.

Level 2B: Illustrative Tasks

High (65%–90%).   Tend copier machine; place material on screen; add paper if necessary; rotate dials and/or press buttons for number of copies, collation, and/or reduction functions; check quality of copy; and pick up copies from bin, following SOP *in order to* produce duplicated materials. (SWB)

Tend a folding machine that folds flyers and similar material for insertion into mailers and adjusts machine as necessary, following SOP *in order to* produce large quantities of inserts for distribution. (SWB)

Oversee the production of mailing labels for different departments, filling in for absent operators if necessary; monitor the operation of computers; and check that printer is loaded with the proper material, following SOP *in order to* produce requested mailing labels. (SVA)

Medium (35%–60%).   Put the mail through the stamp machine after setting the machine for the appropriate stamp price, weighing letters that seem to call for more than the basic rate, following SOP *in order to* mail out items. (SWB)

Key into computer on monthly basis the amounts of office supplies used during the month, recording information on special disk containing office supply inventory data, following SOP *in order to* have an up-to-date inventory and source for what needs to be ordered. (SWB)

Low (5%–30%).   Write checks manually, enter into computer data relating to in-house payments that are circumstantial (e.g., travel advances) or that have not been generated by the normal routine, first checking by phone whether "emergency" is real and manual issuance is necessary, relying on experience *in order to* issue checks for emergency and normal operations. (APS)

Things Level 3A: Manipulating

Definition.   Works (cuts, shapes, assembles, etc.), digs, moves, guides, or places objects or materials where objects, tools, controls, and so on, are several in number. Precision requirements range from gross to fine. Includes waiting on tables and the use of ordinary portable power tools with interchangeable parts and ordinary tools around the home such as kitchen and garden tools used for food preparation, installation, and minor repairs.

Comments.   There are some cases in which a miscellany of simple actions can be grouped under a single collective task. For tasks that involve service and maintenance (e.g., handyman, secretarial, janitorial), it is possible to break out each action as a separate task, but such a degree of description needs to be balanced against the practical purpose for which the analysis is conducted. This judgment is similar to the admonition that time and motion type of analyses should be avoided.

Level 3A: Illustrative Tasks

High (65%–90%).   Arrange office furniture such as desks, tables, and chairs; hang bulletin boards; paint walls as requested, relying on lifting ability and cooperativeness *in order to* have offices set up and ready for use. (HVD)

Drill/dig out holes for lock, throw, and strike plate, on both door and jamb, using portable power drill, drilling jig, and hand tools such as chisel and hammer, following SOP *in order to* prepare for lock assembly. (HST)

Install ¼" plywood panels over window or door areas where glass has been broken, observe condition of wood, cut to size with 1" overlap completely around space being covered, and fasten with screws, using electric screw shooter and hand tools, following SOP *in order to* prevent breaking of glass and unlocking doors and windows from inside. (HST)

Clean/adjust and carry out specified preventative maintenance of computer hardware, using cleaning fluid and cans of compressed air to blow out dust accumulations, drawing on knowledge of computer equipment and understanding of maintenance requirements *in order to* maintain the equipment in working order. (SYA)

Service center van: check oil, transmission fluid, and air in tires, clean inside and outside of vehicle; and keep mileage records, following SOP *in order to* insure van is in operating condition. (HVD)

Medium (35%–60%).   Inventory classroom supplies and materials, using special inventory forms; order new materials as needed for upcoming semester; clean materials before packing, label major equipment and furniture; and store materials over school breaks, following SOP *in order to* have materials and supplies available for following school year. (HST)

Low (5%–30%).   Package/box requisitioned supplies, with assistance of youth worker, selecting items from shelves as called for, relying on attention to detail, and following SOP *in order to* deliver supplies requested. (SWB)

(See page 72 for additional Manipulating tasks)

Things Level 3B: Operating-Controlling I

Definition.   Starts, stops, controls, and adjusts a machine or equipment designed to fabricate and/or process things, data, or people. The worker may be involved in activating the machine, as in word processing or turning wood, or the involvement may occur primarily at startup and stop as with a semi-automatic machine. Operating a machine involves readying and adjusting the machine and/or material as work progresses. Controlling equipment involves monitoring gauges, dials, and so on, and turning valves and other devices to control such items as temperature, pressure, flow of liquids, speed of pumps, and reaction of materials. (This rating is applied only to operators of one machine or one unit of equipment)

Comments.   Jobs rated for this function will often involve enough Data for them be rated almost as high for Data as for Things. As a result, there will not be many examples of Operating-Controlling benchmarks with a high orientation rating. The same will be true for Set-up.

The same phenomenon will be observed in the People scale. As the functions ascend the scale they involve more and more Data.

Level 3B: Illustrative Tasks

High (65–90%).

Medium(35%–60%). Operate/check agency computer system each day, keying in codes to access specific screens that display disk capacity, memory usage, printer usage, and security violations, drawing on knowledge of computer system and relying on keyboard skills *in order to* check for violations or signs of usage danger (e.g., approach to overcapacity). (SYA)

Generate a computer printout of accounts payable for all accounts, check with Accounts Payable Clerk as to why certain items are still on the list, and contact relevant program individuals for clearance as appropriate, drawing on knowledge of agency accounting system and following SOP *in order to* reconcile accounts payable. (ACT)

Oversee the production of computer copies of payroll, accounts payable, and purchase orders on a weekly and bi-weekly basis, libraries (directories) on a daily basis, and entire system on a weekly basis, using both reels and disks and assisting in computer operation as necessary, drawing on knowledge of agency accounting system and relying on computer skills, following SOP *in order to* produce back up copies of vital data. (SYA)

Turn/open gate valves on boiler to release water, sediments, and steam at water column at front of boiler daily for 3 seconds and at back of boiler 3 times weekly for 10 seconds, drawing on knowledge and experience with boiler system and relying on attention to detail following SOP *in order to* clear out sediments from boiler. (JAN)

Position/adjust dies in power press, using wrench, clamping sheet of material onto machine bed; turn on power and depress pedal that forces cutting die through sheet, drawing on knowledge of machine and job orders and relying on attention to detail *in order to* obtain article of specified size and shape. (PPR)

Low (5%-30%).

Things Level 3C: Driving—Controlling

Definition.   Starts, stops, and controls (steers, guides) the actions of machines in two-dimensional space for which a course must be followed to move things or people. Actions regulating controls require continuous attention and readiness of response to surface traffic conditions.

Comments.   Safety is particularly vital to this function because others beside the operator or driver can be endangered. Safety rules and regulations are intertwined throughout the knowledge and abilities associated with this function.

Level 3C: Illustrative Tasks

High (65%–90%).   Drive van to work site in sequence determined by supervisor on basis of convenience to clients, drawing on experience as vehicle operator and knowledge of city traffic patterns *in order to* reach destination on schedule. (HST)

Drive van to stores (hardware, grocery) loading pre-ordered supplies (e.g., cakes, helium tanks) into van *in order to* deliver supplies to appropriate site when needed. (HVD)

Drive small battery-operated delivery van through hallways and between buildings of a hospital, stopping at designated locations, drawing on knowledge of safe van-operating guidelines *in order to* pick up and load containers of dirty laundry into van for delivery to washing room. (TBE)

Drive bus along prescribed route, stopping at designated addresses at scheduled times, calling on clients, and assisting them to the bus if necessary *in order to* bring clients to center for treatment. (TBE)

Medium (35%–60%).   Drive automatic shift van between the Community Center and the Family Crisis Shelter; wait for staff and parents to bring the children to the van, going into the center to inform receptionist that the Head Start Van has arrived for pick-up as necessary; assist the children into the van; buckle their seat belts; lock the doors, check off names on attendance sheet, adding names and starting dates of new students as appropriate, following SOP *in order to* safely transport children to the Head Start site from the Family Crisis Center. (HVD)

Low (5%–30%).   Seek out/contact particular gang or individuals who have been reported as making trouble or on the verge of trouble, while cruising neighbourhood by car or on foot *in order to* explore with them the opportunities for diversion. (STW)

Things Level 3D: Starting Up

Definition.   Prepares/readies powered mobile equipment for operation, typically following standard procedures. Manipulates controls to start up engines, allows for warm-up and pressure build-up as necessary, checks mobility where movement is involved and working parts such as brakes, and gauges indicating serviceability (fuel, pressure, temperature, battery output, etc.), and visually checks for leaks and other unusual conditions. Includes reverse shut-down procedures.

Comments.   Start-up procedures tend to be standardized routines that are basically the same regardless of equipment used.

Level 3D: Illustrative Tasks

High (65%–90%). Start and warm up dozer upon receipt of work order, test raising and lowering of blade, check gauges, followed by final visual check of entire machine for fluid leaks or damaged or worn parts, drawing on experience and following SOP *in order to* have equipment ready to begin work. (BUO)

Prepare/adjust assembly machine, aligning parts, guides, and actuators; adjusting air pressure and sensors as required; drawing on knowledge of assembly process, machine operation, maintenance and set-up procedures, safety procedures and guidelines; and relying on mechanical and problem-solving ability, discretion, and attention to detail *in order to* have assembly machine ready for production. (MFM)

Start and warm up grader upon receipt of work order, placing controls in neutral; apply parking brake; move throttle to ¼ speed; check gauges; test controls; and conduct final equipment check, drawing on experience and following SOP *in order to* have equipment ready for work. (GRA)

Start and warm up backhoe upon assignment in accordance with manufacturer's specifications, check gauges and tests controls as necessary, followed by a final visual check of entire machine for problems that have developed since start up, drawing on experience *in order to* ensure that equipment is ready for operation. (BH0)

Medium (35%–60%).

Low (5%–30%).

Things Level 4A: Precision Working

Definition.   Works, moves, guides, or places objects or materials according to standard practical procedures where the number of objects, materials, tools, and so on, embraces an entire craft and accuracy expected is within final finished tolerances established for the craft. (Use this rating where work primarily involves manual or power hand tools.)

Comments.   Tasks at the Precision Working level typically require an orientation to Data almost or equal to the Things orientation.

Level 4A: Illustrative Tasks

High (65%–90%). Cut/mitre framing material in mitre jig, using either manual or powered saw, drawing on specifications of work order, knowledge of angle required for cut, characteristics of assorted framing materials (e.g., hardwood, plastic, metal) and relying on ability to use hand and power tools, patience, and attention to detail *in order to* ready materials for frame assembly. (FRM)

Medium (35%–60%). Manipulate/arrange broken bones in damaged limb, applying splints and wrappings; drawing on medical knowledge, training, and experience; and relying on interpersonal and kinesthetic skill *in order to* set bones in natural position for healing. (TBE)

Draft full-size or scale detail drawings of either autobody or chassis parts and assemblies, using drafting instruments and work aids; drawing on specifications, master drawings, layouts, models, prototypes, sketches and/or verbal instructions, methods of manufacture; and relying on spatial relations and drawing skills and attention to detail *in order to* prepare drawings for engineering and manufacturing purposes. (ADD)

Draw/paint commercial illustrations, using assorted paints, brushes, media materials, lettering devices, drawing on layouts, sketches of proposed illustrations, and related materials and relying on personal aesthetics, styles, and techniques *in order to* produce illustrations for use by various media to explain or adorn printed or spoken word. (ILL)

Low (5%–30%). Test water from boiler system for temporary hardness, permanent hardness, total hardness, pH-Hydrogen Ion, Sulfite M6-L, "p", alkalinity, chlorides, condensate, and total dissolved solids, using chemistry set, treating boiler with chemicals to bring solvent levels up to specifications, drawing on knowledge of chemistry involved and boiler system, and relying on attention to detail *in order to* maintain water solvent levels. (JAN)

Things Level 4B: Setting Up

Definition.　　Installs machines or equipment; inserts tools; alters jigs, fixtures, and attachments and/or repairs machines or equipment to ready and/or restore them to their proper functioning according to job order or blueprint specifications. Involves primary responsibility for accuracy. May involve one or a number of machines for other workers or worker's own operations.

Comments.　　There is a wide range of job–worker situations in industry in regard to Operating-Controlling and Setting Up machines. This range relates to the level of difficulty and consequent need for training and experience. On the most complex level is the need to set up multiple machines that are similar or of varying type. This fulfills the definition for Setting Up. At a simpler level are the job–worker situations where workers set up and operate one machine. This meets the definition for Operating-Controlling. On a still simpler level are machine-tending, job–worker situations where workers tend the machines readied by those rated for setting up. Within each of these three categorized levels there is also a range of difficulty that does not lend itself to reliable discrimination.

Most setting-up tasks involve an equally high involvement with data.

Level 4B: Illustrative Tasks

High (65%–90%).   Install new PC equipment at remote sites, using basic tools as needed; connecting network server, monitor keyboard, modems, printer, and surge protector; and introducing related software, sometimes setting up a separate directory for a major application, checking out the installation on a test case to see if it works, drawing on experience and knowledge of computer operations, and relying on attention to detail *in order to* provide client with necessary data processing equipment. (SYA)

Medium (35%–60%).   Design a computer program from scratch (e.g., food service program), where the existing data are not well organized in manual files; write a program that processes the data as requested; test the program on a sample problem; review results with end user and modify as necessary, drawing on programming experience and knowledge of content area communicated by department SMEs, relying on analytical skill and persistence *in order to* produce a program that meets the needs of the end user. (SYA)

Adjust/install dies in punch presses, using wrench and press gauge to adjust guide stops as required, drawing on knowledge of punch press operation, maintenance and adjustment procedures, plant safety requirements, production tolerances, and statistical process control (SPC) targets and relying on individual discretion *in order to* have machine set up for production of parts within quality tolerance standards. (PPO)

Low (5%–30%).   Oversee installation of mainframe computer system units, deciding on and supervising the positioning of units by other personnel, and making trial computer runs to sort out start-up problems with reference to blueprints and layout specifications, drawing on personal experience *in order to* ensure operation of new computer center. (TBE)

(See pages 72–73 for additional Setting Up tasks)

Things Level 4C: Operating—Controlling II

Definition. Starts, stops, controls, and continuously modifies set-up of equipment designed to hoist and move materials or transport persons and/or materials in multidimensional space; includes the operation of heavy equipment to reshape and/or pave the earth's surface. Manipulation of controls requires continuous attention to changing conditions and readiness of response to activate the equipment in lateral, vertical, and/or angular operations.

Comments. Tasks at the Operating-Controlling II level typically involve the continuous processing of information based on experience, as much as on physical handling of control devices. The analyst should be careful not to overrate the percentage orientation to Things.

Level 4C: Illustrative Tasks

High (65%–90%).

Medium (35%–60%). Operate a backhoe, manipulating controls to move forward/back, turn/swing, boom up/down, telescope and move bucket; monitor the performance of the equipment and adapt to changing work conditions; alert to presence and safety of other workers/equipment, following work orders, specifications, stakes, hand signals, laser beam, or string line; drawing on personal knowledge of and experience with various makes/models of backhoe, job situations, and work requirements and relying on personal judgment *in order to* carry out precision excavation, place riprap, or pipe. (BHO)

Operate a crane, manipulating controls to travel forward/backward, swing, boom up/down, telescope in/out (if hydraulic), or trolley in/out (if lower type); monitor the performance of the equipment and adapt to changing work conditions; alert to presence and safety of people and equipment, following work orders and/or hand/radio signals; drawing on knowledge of proper crane operation, safety requirements, and experience with specific make and type of crane and relying on own judgment in determining maneuvers appropriate to load, size, and weight *in order to* hoist material, erect steel, or pour concrete. (CRO)

Operate a crane with a clamshell attachment, manipulating controls to travel forward/backward, swing, boom up/down, raise, lower, and open/close bucket; monitor equipment performance and adapt to changing work conditions; alert to the presence and safety of people and equipment, drawing on knowledge of and experience with equipment and type of work *in order to* stack or pile earth, brush, or trees. (CRO)

Low (5%–30%).

(See page 73 for additional Operating—Controlling II tasks)

Additional Illustrative Tasks: Things Functions

Level 1A: Handling

High.   Vacuum/mop carpeted areas and floors, using vacuum cleaner and wet/dry mop, wiping desks, tables, counters, blackboards, front door windows, and walls as needed, and emptying waste baskets and ash trays into trash containers, following SOP *in order to* clean rooms in building on a daily basis. (JAN)

Load/unload donations (mattresses, clothes) from trucks, vans, or cars, carrying them to designated areas such as clients' homes, crisis centers, and homeless housing programs, drawing on knowledge of safe lifting procedures and relying on physical strength, following SOP *in order to* deliver donations to appropriate place. (JAN)

Remove basket strainers from accumulator tank on a weekly basis, dump strained solids into barrel, and then brush, clean, and rinse strainer, relying on experience and following SOP in order to clean baskets. (JNP)

Arrange/place office supplies in designated places in storage cabinet, relying on attention to detail and following SOP *in order to* make supplies available to staff. (SWB)

Low.   Visit employers, referring to newspaper want ads and cold phone calls and posting located job openings, drawing on reading, verbal, and interpersonal skills, as well as personal initiative *in order to* open up job and training opportunities for unemployed youth and youth at risk. (STW)

Level 3A: Manipulating

High.   Oversee/supervise children in walking down stairs, holding onto rails, getting to gym or outside play yard, engaging them in structured (walking balance beam, tumbling, bouncing and catching ball) and free-choice (run, ride bikes, play basketball, climbing) physical activities, drawing on knowledge of gross motor skills and their role in childhood growth *in order to* promote gross motor development and cooperative play. (HST)

Prepare/decorate classroom setting with colored construction paper, picture cutouts, corrugated paper, thematic materials relating to learning areas specified in federal guidelines (e.g., nutrition, science, health, emergency procedures, music, multiculture), bulletin boards (library, parent news), and learning materials, drawing on federal guidelines and aesthetic interests and relying on personal initiative and decorative ability *in order to* design a colorful, stimulating, well-balanced environment. (HDT)

Level 4B: Setting Up

Medium. Repair/recondition control valves, using hand tools and appropriate solvents, cleaning valve parts of all residue, and replacing gaskets/seals and parts as necessary, drawing on knowledge of valve types and operation, manufacturers' specifications, and dismantle/assembly procedures and relying on mechanical aptitude, problem-solving ability, and attention to detail *in order to* prepare valves for pressure testing and return to operation. (PIP)

Adjust/align grinding wheel of automated parts grinder, moving spindle assembly as necessary to obtain proper tracking, dressing grind stone with diamond wheel for fit to grind template, drawing on knowledge of grinder operation and adjustment procedures, safety procedures and regulations, parts specifications, and experience of self and coworkers and relying on attention to detail and individual discretion *in order to* return grinding machine to specifications for production of quality parts. (GRM)

Set up an experimental situation (laboratory or field), using existing supplies and modifying them as necessary, requisitioning equipment needed to simulate a computer display, collecting the performance measures with or without the aid of technicians, drawing on technical knowledge of the equipment and the particular type of display being researched, and relying on management skills *in order to* have an experimental situation that allows for an assessment of the various options being explored. (HFI)

Level 4C Operating: Controlling II

Medium. Operate bulldozer, manipulating controls to crawl forward/back, raise/lower/tilt/angle blade; monitor the performance of equipment and adapt to changing work conditions; alert to the presence and safety of other workers/equipment, following work orders, grade, stakes or other work specifications; drawing on personal knowledge, experience, and own assessment of best method to get the job done *in order to* carry out critical, hazardous work such as clearing, pioneering, demolition, winching, or finish work such as ditching, sloping, or building/cutting trenches. (DUO)

Operate grader, manipulating controls to travel forward/back, turn, raise/lower blade, position wheels and blade at correct angles; monitor the performance of the equipment and adapt to changing work conditions; alert to presence and safety of other workers/equipment, following work orders, grade stakes or other work specifications; drawing on knowledge and experience *in order to* blend materials, spread, and do rough crowning, ditching, grading, and road shoulder maintenance (GRA)

DATA FUNCTIONS SCALE

Data should be understood to mean information, ideas, facts, and statistics. Involvement with Data is inherent in the simplest job instruction in the form of recognizing the relationship of a tool to its function or the significance of a pointing instruction. Data are always present in a task, even though the major emphasis of the task might be dealing with Things and/or People. Where Things are primarily involved, Data tend to show up as specifications. Where People are primarily involved, Data tend to show up as information about objective events or conditions, information about feelings, or ideas that could be tinged with objective information and/or feeling. The Data Scale measures the degree to which workers might be expected to become involved with Data in the tasks they are asked to perform, from simple recognition through degrees of arranging, executing, and modifying to reconceptualizing Data.

The data functions in work and learning are the same, but there is an important difference. In work situations the functions tend to be demarcated and allocated to specific assignments reflecting organization structure and production flow. In the learning situation, functions know no bounds. Every new learning can be a challenge involving aspects of creativity (synthesizing) and, hence, all subsidiary functions in the Data scale—either slowly or quickly. Thus, the Data scale basically reflects the cognitive development that occurs in human learning.

Data are information, ideas, facts, statistics, specification of output, knowledge of conditions, techniques, and mental operations.

The arabic number assigned to definitions represents the successive levels of this ordinal scale. The A, B, C, and D definitions are variations on the same level.

Data Benchmarks

Level 1: Comparing

Definition.   Selects, sorts, or arranges data, people, or things, judging whether their readily observable functional, structural, or compositional characteristics are similar to or different from prescribed standards. Examples: checks oil level, tire pressure, worn cables; observes and responds to hand signal of worker indicating movement of load; sizes, sorts, and culls tangibles being conveyed to workers; compares lists of names and numbers for similarity.

Comments.   In FJA, the Things, Data, and People functions are conceived as emerging from the two basic, across-the-board functions, Observing and Learning. Comparing emerges as the initial Data function from this base. It is closely associated with the cognitive process of establishing identities and naming things, perceiving similarities and differences. When the similarities and differences pertain to names and numbers it is called *clerical perception*; when it pertains to tangibles/things it is called *form perception*; when it pertains to mechanical devices it is called *spatial perception*. All other Data functions build on this foundation.

Level I: Ilustrative Tasks

High (65%–90%).   Match/compare routine and blanket invoices/bills with receiving reports and purchase orders (e.g., fuel for vehicles, hardware), following SOP *in order to* insure that payment is made in agreement with vendor invoices and/or statements. (APS)

Check computer printout of purchase requisition against original information, following SOP *in order to* insure that information entered into computer is as originally approved and to initiate purchase order. (PUA)

Retrieve purchase orders produced by Data Department, sorts for amount, giving special attention to orders that require dual signatures, following SOP *in order to* sign off on purchase orders. (PUA)

Check time cards for completeness and for approvals of overtime by executive director, relying on attention to detail and following SOP *in order to* insure that they are signed by both employee and supervisor. (PSS)

Review/scan a computer printout of payroll hours entries for details such as no more than 80 hours per person per pay period, correctness of account numbers assigned for time worked, and improper rates of pay, drawing on experience with and knowledge of agency payroll classifications and program allocations and relying on sense of how the printout should look *in order to* insure that payroll is correct and to identify items requiring further analysis. (CAT)

Medium (35%–60%).   Collate selected documents by hand that cannot be handled by machine, following specifications and relying on manual skills *in order to* produce an assembled product. (SWB)

Sort mail into mail boxes, reading the names off envelopes, speeding the sort by recognition of the types of envelopes (i.e., bills, bank statements, announcements), separating out mail that needs to be returned to postal station because of wrong address *in order to* have mail ready for pick up by addressees. (SWB)

Check tires, turn on headlights, signals, wipers, and warning lights daily, drawing on knowledge of vehicle operation *in order to* make sure van is in safe working condition. (HVD)

Low (5%–30%).   Review/scan room set-up with reference to the day's lesson plan for furniture arrangement, materials, and supplies, removing chairs from tables and wiping tables down *in order to* insure that equipment and materials are available for day's planned activities. (HST)

Data Level 2: Copying

Definition.   Transcribes, enters, and/or posts data, following a schema or plan to assemble or make things, using a variety of work aids. Transfers information mentally from plans, diagrams, instructions to work piece or work site. Examples: attends to stakes showing a grade line to be followed while operating equipment.

Comments.   Copying can be either mental, physical, or interpersonal as in mimicking. However, it starts as a mental perception and depends on the aptitude for matching names and numbers (clerical perception) for much of its effectiveness.

Level 2: Illustrative Tasks

High (65%–90%).   Log/note on form provided data relating to long distance calls (e.g., caller, party called, number), following SOP *in order to* insure that calls will be charged to appropriate budget. (SWB)

Complete a receiving report when requisitioned material arrives, note requested information such as quantity and condition, attach report to invoice, and forward it to accounts payable, following SOP *in order to* have supplies/materials paid for. (SWB)

Note reservations and changes on yearly calendar regarding availability of conference rooms, drawing on changes called in by manager of administration and staff and relying on attention to detail, following SOP *in order to* inform people of changes in meeting time and place. (SWB)

Add/remove names on committee membership files when informed by supervisor, relying on attention to detail *in order to* keep files current and to insure proper distribution of files to committee. (SWB)

Medium (35%–60%).   Assign a serial number for new vendors when informed of their selection by a program area, keying number, identification, and conditions of payment into computer, following SOP *in order to* facilitate payments. (APS)

Post accounting transactions into accounting system daily, drawing on knowledge of agency system, computer software, and relying on attention to detail *in order to* update system and keep information current. (CAT)

Key the data obtained on medical social work and diagnostic medical screening interview forms into computer, copying the data according to an established program *in order to* establish a central data bank for clients. (SWF)

Low (5%–30%).   Install metal burglar bars, conduit (telescoped ¾" to 1" pipe), or angle aluminum on windows to meet different situations (e.g., burglar bars on first floor windows or windows that are nailed down), drilling holes according to template and driving screws to secure bars or using rivet in case of conduit, drawing on work order specifications and experience and following SOP *in order to* burglar proof the residence. (HST)

Clear paper jam in copying machine following specified procedure built into machine, adding toner, staple wire, and paper when called for, and cleaning the feeder with cotton dipped in alcohol *in order to* return machine to running order. (SWB)

(See page 92 for additional Copying tasks)

Data Level 3A: Computing

Definition.   Performs arithmetic operations and makes reports and/or carries out a prescribed action in relation to them. Interprets mathematical data on plans, specifications, diagrams, or blueprints, transferring them to workpiece; for example, reads and follows specifications on stakes.

Comments.   Computing became a designated function before (1950) computers were in wide use. The definition has not changed and applies strictly to the processing of numbers and mathematical symbols. Computer operation as such is a machine function and accounted for by functions in the Things hierarchy. The level of difficulty of the numbers and symbols processed is accounted for in the Math hierarchy of the GED scales.

Helpful Hints.   It is not necessary to indicate "relying on basic arithmetic skills" where basic arithmetic is obvious in the task. The appropriate mathematical skill should be indicated when more complex mathematical skills are involved, such as basic statistics, algebra, and trigonometry.

Level 3A: Illustrative Tasks

High (65%–90%). Calculate advanced earned income payments (taxes) for qualified employees who complete form W-5, drawing on knowledge of mandated federal tax guidelines and following SOP *in order to* fulfill requests of employees. (PSS)

Calculate/compute client billing, using standard formula and calculator as necessary, drawing on administration manual *in order to* bill client and avoid financial errors. (PSR)

Multiply estimated daily travel by number of working/training days in month, using calculator as necessary, drawing on knowledge of transportation systems and local geography *in order to* record monthly travel allowance of client in training program. (TBE)

Add/total figures in income categories on public assistance application form, drawing on knowledge of agency SOP *in order to* record gross family income. (TBE)

Calculate percentages of grant allocated for rent, utilities, food, and clothing, using calculator as necessary, drawing on prescribed budget formula, and relying on basic statistical skill *in order to* check/record distribution of money among budget categories. (TBE)

Medium (35%–60%).

Low (5%–30%).

Data Level 3B: Compiling

Definition.   Gathers, collates, or classifies information about things, data, or people, following schema or system, but using discretion in application. Examples: considers wind, weather (rain or shine), shape, weight and type of load, height, and capacity of boom in making lift using a crane; converts information in a book (title, author, subject, etc.) into a standard library code.

Level 3B: Illustrative Tasks

High (65%–90%). Fill in/complete forms and assign voucher number for approved bills and invoices (e.g., lease payments, consultant fees, utilities, travel advances), following agency accounting procedure and SOP *in order to* enter information into computer for issuance of checks. (APS)

Prepare/list a monthly accounts payable exception list (problem accounts), noting outstanding accounts and missing paper for forwarding to agency administrators, relying on attention to detail and following SOP *in order to* keep administrators updated on programs that are not on track. (APS)

Access applicant data records, manually compiling data specifics relevant to requests from state and county governments regarding the implementation of affirmative action (e.g., race, sex, age, veteran status) *in order to* fulfill the report requirements of state and county governments. (PSU)

Accumulate/compile data on needs of low-income energy assistance applicants, including energy costs and population characteristics, drawing on previous proposals, recently developed data in government reports and case files *in order to* bring the grant proposal up to date. (PIS)

Medium (35%–60%). Attend staff and seminar meetings, sharing information and experience as well as absorbing material presented *in order to* stay informed about what is going on in agency and to acquire new skills and knowledge. (PSS)

Attend courses, workshops, and other educational activities dealing with legal services, youth and community resources, drawing on educational background and agency support and relying on personal initiative *in order to* acquire additional information on current theory and practice that could be useful. (IRS)

Low (5%–30%). Present/talk to groups of students or individuals in high schools, middle schools, and/or alternative schools on request from human relations personnel in school, sorting and gathering material designed to motivate students to stay in school and to avoid potentially criminal situations, drawing on materials and training provided by agency and relying on personal style, initiative, life experience, and rapport with students *in order to* make an impression and to describe personal availability to give help. (STW)

(See page 92 for additional Compiling tasks)

Data Level 4: Analyzing

Definition. Examines and evaluates data (about things, data, or people) with reference to the criteria, standards, and/or requirements of a particular discipline, art, technique, or craft to determine interaction effects (consequences) and to consider alternatives. Examples: considers/ evaluates instructions, site and climatic conditions, nature of load, capacity of equipment, other crafts engaged with in order to situate (spot) a crane to best advantage; researches a problem in a particular subject matter area to consider and enumerate the options available in dealing with it.

Comments. This function reflects a major objective of the educational process—the ability to evaluate accumulated data about a subject or issue in terms of the options offered and the consequences of actions taken in relation to those options. The education can, of course, be acquired in schools as well as from experience or both. Learning to analyze is at the heart of the mastery of a craft or profession.

Level 4: Illustrative Tasks

High (65%–90%). Examine/evaluate employment data obtained from protected groups, using statistical programs on computer, drawing on the standard procedures outlined in Equal Employment Opportunity Commission (EEOC) guidelines for assessing differential validity and test bias, psychometrics, statistics, and relying on mathematical and analytical skills *in order to* determine whether selection instruments demonstrate adverse impact. (IOP)

Read/evaluate various methods of conducting research of a problem, drawing on the statistical, theoretical, and methodological literature related to problem, personal knowledge and experience, and/or advice of colleagues and relying on problem-solving ability *in order to* choose a methodology that is practical, feasible, and appropriate. (ARP)

Evaluate training, drawing on ratings obtained from trainees on special forms prepared for the purpose, including such factors as trainer preparation and skill, coverage of content, special materials, learning facilities, and trainee's perceived level of achievement, relying on basic statistical skills *in order to* determine the effectiveness of the training and accomplishment of objectives. (TRS)

Read/review monthly reports sent by directors of delegate agency, checking their compliance on such matters as enrollment, waiting lists, health and dental information, drawing on the requirements of the federal guidelines and relying on reading comprehension skills *in order to* insure that they are meeting funded enrollment and providing required services. (HSA)

Medium (35%–60%). Take pictures, mainly black and white, on own initiative or on request from program people, using either a 35mm camera or a second camera containing color film, framing, and focusing pictures with attention to aesthetic and interest characteristics, and with relevance to the particular story being covered, relying on experience and artistic skills *in order to* illustrate articles, brochures, and special events. (PIS)

Low (5%–30%). Assess/screen children entering Head Start program, using test kits that measure motor abilities (large and small), cognition, and language abilities, drawing on special training in test administration and relying on interpersonal skills with children *in order to* identify child's special needs (visual, speech, motor) and to provide baseline assessment information for each child's Individual Education Plan (IEP). (HST)

(See page 92 for additional Analyzing tasks)

Data Level 5A: Innovating

Definition.   Modifes, alters, and/or adapts existing designs, procedures, or methods to meet unique specifications, unusual conditions, or specific standards of effectiveness within the overall framework of operating theories, principles, and/or organizational contexts; for example, improvises, using existing attachments, or modifies customary equipment to meet unusual conditions and fulfill specifications.

Comments.   Innovating is the function that business and industry are mostly seeking when they talk about "creativity." Innovating can be effectively managed within the customary structure of organizations. It is possible to order, direct, specify, and manage innovation—unlike true creativity.

Helpful Hint.   Tasks concerned with creativity are associated with the synthesizing, rather than the innovating, function of the Data scale.

Level 5A: Illustrative Tasks

High (65%–90%). Document/report dysfunctions or new financial requirements, modify procedures to overcome short-term dysfunctions and meet new requirements, drawing on the assistance of chief accountants, knowledge of computerized accounting system, software specifications, and the new requirements, and relying on personal ingenuity *in order to* maintain integrity of the system until correction or redesign is available. (CTR)

Develop/design user interface, including the selection and arrangement of controls/displays, messages, workplace layout, colors, warnings, and labeling, using and/or adapting existing designs; drawing on databases, legal requirements, national/international standards, and related resources; and relying on computer design skills *in order to* meet product requirements and to produce a user-friendly product. (HFC)

Review/rewrite refunding proposals for community programs, drawing on preexisting proposals, projected changes in the program, and funding service specifications and relying on writing skills and experience in preparing proposals *in order to* secure continued funding for the specified program. (PSC)

Develop training needs questionnaire for distribution to agency staff using existing questionnaires, adapting them to particular considerations such as how the questionnaire will be understood by respondents and the manner in which the data will be compiled, drawing on knowledge of agency and relying on training experience *in order to* generate data for an agencywide training plan. (TRS)

Medium (35%-60%). Meet with personnel concerned about policy and procedural issues, including financial operations, and conduct a brain-storming session on proposed revisions, drawing on knowledge of issue and relying on communication skills and sensitivity to proposals made *in order to* develop revised recommendations on policy, procedure, or methods of operation. (CTR)

Conduct workshops for parents and staff, using previous lesson plans, adapting material to the needs of the participants, drawing on knowledge of nutrition and relying on instructional skills *in order to* insure that staff and parents are equipped to make informed food choices. (HSN)

Low (5%–30%).

(See page 93 for additional Innovating tasks)

Data Level 5B: Coordinating

Definition. Decides times, place, and sequence of operations of a process, system, or organization, and/or the need for revision of goals, policies (boundary conditions), or procedures on the basis of analysis of data and of performance review of pertinent objectives and requirements. Includes overseeing and/or executing decisions and/or reporting on events; for example, selects/proposes equipment best suited to achieve an output considering resources (equipment, costs, personnel) available to get the job done.

Comments. Coordinating is the quintessential management function. It is the function that represents management decision making and balancing with reference to the Data (Information and Ideas) that it has to work with. The decisions are implemented in the areas of Things and People as well as Data.

Level 5B: Illustrative Tasks

High (65%–90%). Plan/schedule a series of group sessions of substance abuse counsellors to work with shelter clients, drawing on social work background, professional status, and relying on personal initiative and management skills *in order to* have counselors teach shelter clients how to deal with substance abuse as a family problem. (SWF)

Prepare/write an integrated report for the regional office of Head Start, reading, summarizing, and highlighting activities and developments, and indicating plans for resolving problems; drawing on the monthly and quarterly reports and progress indicators of both agency and delegate Head Start programs and relying on writing and organization skills *in order to* keep the funding source up to date and informed. (HSA)

Medium (35%–60%). Meet/discuss performance with top subordinate staff, one-on-one, reviewing with them progress made in achieving personal goals for the year, problems encountered if any (e.g., with subordinate personnel, or with equipment), training and/or self-development undertaken, innovations introduced, and goals for the coming year, drawing on mutual experience, documentation of recorded incidents, and agency evaluation procedures and relying on interpersonal skills and sensitivity *in order to* carry out an annual performance appraisal. (CTR)

Conduct bimonthly Health and Nutrition committee meetings with Health Coordinator, set agenda, arrange for space and for speakers, prepare materials, disseminate information, and network with community resources, drawing on knowledge of the organization and relying on communication and management skills *in order to* exchange information and keep up to date. (HSN)

Schedule and conduct an interview in response to a call from within agency about an ongoing program or event, obtaining the facts, drawing on personal knowledge of relevant people, and understanding of the situation, and relying on an awareness of which media should be used to promote the story, as well as writing and interviewing skills *in order to* prepare a written article describing the program or event. (PIS)

Low (5%–30%).

(See pages 93–94 for additional Coordinating tasks)

Data Level 6: Synthesizing

Definition. Takes off in new directions on the basis of personal intuitions, feelings, and ideas (with or without regard for tradition, experience, and existing parameters) to conceive new approaches to or statements of problems and the development of system, operational or aesthetic solutions, or resolutions of them, typically outside of existing theoretical, stylistic, or organizational context.

Comments. Synthesizing is the "creativity" function, intensely personal and individual. It is a Data function not easily understood, managed, or tolerated in many organizational contexts.

The tasks that follow are not likely to appear in job analysis inventories of organizations in the same way as tasks for all other functions. They are more or less descriptions by creative people of what they do in the creative process. However, they are not prescriptive. There is no inevitable logic or rationale that leads to creativity. The creative act has defied analysis and predictability.

Level 6: Illustrative Tasks

High (65%–90%). Conceive/intuit/explore relationships among selected theories and techniques from outside social work discipline, and integrate them with accepted social work practice, relying on research and writing skills and previous social work experience *in order to* develop/test a new problem-solving process for multiproblem family. (TBE)

Conceptualize/intuit new relationships between existing and evolving analytic theories and techniques without documented precedents, relating them to organizational problems, drawing on an understanding of theory and conceptual models, and relying on personal insights, experience, and analytical and writing skills *in order to* develop an approach and methodology for a demonstration project or for a research model. (TBE)

Conceive/create an original hypothesis about the nature of social-psychological problems of an ethnic or socioeconomic group, drawing on an understanding of theory and conceptual models and relying on analytical and writing skills *in order to* explain factors and phenomena previously unrecognized or unaccounted for. (TBE)

Read/review articles, reports, papers, and statistical data relevant to agency, whether referred to by staff or discovered on own, taking notes as necessary, drawing on personal background and understanding, and relying on reading comprehension skill *in order to* enhance understanding, discover relationships, and develop materials that contribute to vision and/or provide information for speeches, presentations, or discussions with staff. (EXD)

Medium (35%–60%). Discuss/consult with professional colleagues, students, practitioners, and/or clients about research articles, theoretical literature, and/or ideas derived from professional journals, conference proceedings, books, relying on personal experience and interpersonal and communication skills *in order to* determine areas for research among competing/different theoretical positions. (ARP)

Low (5%–30%).

Additional Illustrative Tasks: Data Functions

Level 2: Copying

High. Visit each agency location, recording serial and property numbers for property valued at $300 or greater onto an inventory form, issuing a property number to those items without one, drawing on knowledge of inventory system *in order to* assist facilities administration in complete annual agencywide inventory. (JAN)

Medium. Prepare/fill out a form for voiding checks issued that have been cancelled or not fulfilled and enter data into computer, drawing on information supplied by vendors or program personnel or when noted as issued incorrectly and following SOP in order to cancel invalid disbursements. (APS)

Level 3B: Compiling

High. Compare/compile checks issued (bank statements) versus checks authorized (accounting records) monthly, searching out discrepancies until complete matching is effected, drawing on knowledge of agency accounting system, and relying on attention to detail *in order to* reconcile issued and authorized checks. (CAT)

Low. Meet weekly one-on-one with lead staff, encouraging their expression of needs, drawing on knowledge of programs and relying on interpersonal skills *in order to* stay informed about what is going on in their programs. (CTD)

Level 4: Analyzing

High. Review/evaluate resumes and/or applications received for a current job opening and prepare a summary report of qualifications of all applicants, drawing on knowledge of job requirements, allowable equivalencies, and relying on writing and computer skills *in order to* determine which applicants meet minimum requirements for the position and can be sent to the hiring supervisor for review. (PSU)

Review applications submitted through the Human Resources Development Office for a staff vacancy, drawing on knowledge of position to be interviewed and agency criteria, following SOP *in order to* select candidates to be interviewed for vacancy and to notify Human Resources Development Office of need to check references. (CAT)

Level 5A: Innovating

High. Develop a course and/or seminar on human factors, including sections on safety, liability, and displays, dividing it into units and adapting it to the requirements of a particular modality (e.g., videotapes, in-person lectures), drawing on existing materials and relying on teaching experience and skills *in order to* educate the professional and technical staff about human factors. (HFI)

Prepare/write a plan (terms of reference, proposal), integrating the results of discussions and decisions about overall approach to be taken, including identification of problem and users, methodology to be used, resources to be drawn on, time frames, critical paths, and sequence of events, and relying on experience and writing skills *in order to* initiate suggested approach. (DBA)

Medium. Modify existing vendor programs, working with department head and/or SME to explore special needs, reviewing the particular files in question, writing, testing, and modifying the revised program as appropriate, relying on programming experience and analytical skills *in order to* meet a special agency need. (SYA)

Level 5B: Coordinating

High. Schedule/oversee the preparation of the programmatic part of a refunding proposal involving the integration of delegate agency proposals and the primary agency portion, drawing on the revised goals and objectives derived from self-assessment validation instruments, progress evaluation and related reports, updated statistical data, a training calendar, and an updated community needs assessment, and relying on planning skills *in order to* justify the attached budget and refunding for the following year. (HSA)

Develop/draft specific plans to address training needs such as information sharing, workshop development, and curriculum development, selecting training resources as appropriate; drawing on knowledge of adult education, nutrition, and community resources; and relying on conceptual and writing skills *in order to* respond to the training requests/needs of parents. (HSN)

Medium. Phone/contact site coordinators and responsible facility contacts (neighborhood centers, schools, churches), arranging specific times and dates for the use of facilities as distribution sites and determining volunteer availability, drawing on long-term relationships and experience with sites and coordinators and relying on communication and management skills *in order to* develop an annual calendar for distributions. (PSC)

Contact site coordinators prior to each food distribution, reviewing issuance rates for households, volunteers, security, forms, supplies, and equipment needed, arranging for visits by census workers and nutrition educators, drawing on knowledge of community resources, site requirements, and needs; relying on interpersonal and management skills *in order to* insure orderly distribution of commodities at all sites. (PSC)

Plan an integrated series of talks by specialists in human services, inviting them to make presentations to assembled clients, drawing on an understanding of client problems and needs and contacts made in the community and relying on personal initiative and communication skills *in order to* inform clients of community facilities and support available to them. (SWF)

PEOPLE FUNCTIONS SCALE

The substance of the live interaction between people (and animals) is communication. In the broadest sense, the communication can be verbal or nonverbal. What makes communication complex is the heavy load that messages carry, for example, Data in their objective and subjective forms—the way in which they are delivered (volume, tone, accompanying gesture, and the formal rules and informal customs that govern the context of the communication). Because there is a large subjective element on the part of both the sender and the receiver of a communication, it is very difficult to measure or to assign absolute values or primary importance to one or another type of information in the interaction.

What further complicates pinning down the nature of specific interpersonal behavior is that *affect* can serve as a *tool* for managing oneself in the interaction as well as the informational *substance* of the interaction. Affect, as information and as tool, can occur in the simplest as well as the most complex interaction. For example, affect expressed in a sulky manner, perhaps to gain attention or perhaps to express resentment on the part of a worker, can quickly become the informational substance of the interaction when the supervisor asks nonreactively, "Don't you feel well?" and gets the answer "No, I don't. My child is ill. I should be home."

The functions in the People scale deal only indirectly with these complex questions. The assumption of ordinality is more tenuous than in the Things and Data scales and depends more heavily on role, status, and authority, which are often associated with, but not necessarily a part of, skill. In effect, the functions try to capture the variety of interpersonal behavior *assigned* in various work situations and are more or less arranged, as in the other scales, according to the need, in general, to deal with increasing numbers of variables and with greater degrees of discretion. (The function least likely to fit this pattern is Supervising, which probably could have a scale of its own.)

Skill in dealing with people is undoubtedly as much an art as a methodology. Although measurement in this area is in a primitive state, it is essential to delineate descriptive and numerical standards by which a function can be appraised in the task in which it occurs. One should especially note cultural boundary conditions in matters of courtesy, diplomatic protocol, and "rule" of behavior in patient-doctor relationships.

The People scale measures live interaction between people, and people and animals.

People Benchmarks

Level 1A: Taking Instructions—Helping

Definition.   Attends to the work assignment, instructions, or orders of supervisor. No immediate response or verbal exchange is required unless clarification of instruction is needed.

Comments.   Several categories of skills are listed as required by the SMEs where there is interpersonal action. On the lower levels they are as follows:

- *Listening:* paying attention to instructions.
- *Practicing courtesy:* showing consideration to people dealt with.
- *Acknowledging:* showing respect for where people are coming from.
- *Communicating orally:* speaking to people clearly.

In the benchmarks that follow, Taking Instructions is largely implicit. Where there is no mention of interpersonal action in a task statement, it is assumed at a minimum, the worker is taking an instruction. It may be that Taking Instructions would only show up as a major interpersonal function in highly structured, military-type situations.

Level 1A: Illustrative Tasks

High (65%–90%).

Medium (35%–60%).

Low (5%–30%).   Move furniture into configurations appropriate for type of meeting (e.g., lecture, seminar), following oral instructions *in order to* have room set up. (JAN)

Approve expenditures up to $300 and countersign expenditures over $300 for accounting department, drawing on authority granted by agency procedures *in order to* comply with agency policies. (CTR)

Rearrange supplies, throwing out unusable items, taking items needing repair to center, and sweeping floors, following oral instructions *in order to* insure supply/storage rooms are orderly. (HVD)

Select final candidate from the joint recommendations of self, deputy director, and Personnel committee, following SOP *in order to* fill the job vacancy. (HSA)

Allocate available foods to participating shelters, feeding sites and pantries, drawing on knowledge of available inventory, number of meals served at each facility, utilization rates, and following SOP *in order to* insure foods are allocated equitably to participating groups. (PSC)

Supply auditors with final printouts and supplementary documentation (e.g., contracts, voucher packages) of financial activities of all programs for calendar year, including special detailed supporting documentation and existing reports (e.g., cash confirmations), drawing on an overall knowledge of accounting system, programs, and customary needs of auditors and relying on cooperativeness *in order to* facilitate the auditing of agency accounts. (CAT)

Review all accounts payable checks for exceptional and unusual payments, drawing on an awareness of agencies with whom agency contracts and relying on attention to detail and experience *in order to* insure that all accounts payable are legitimate. (CTR)

People Level 1B: Serving

Definition.   Attends to the needs or requests of people or animals, or to the expressed or implicit wishes of people. Immediate response is involved.

Comments.   An additional skill mentioned in this context is: Empathy—showing compassion. This skill will continue to show up on higher levels along with increased Data and Interpersonal skills. Analysts should be alert to tasks that require considerable amounts of sensitivity and an awareness of client needs.

Level 1B: Illustrative Tasks

High (65%–90%).   Assist children in getting out of van, walk them to their classroom, give the teacher a copy of any new student forms, and introduce parent(s) of new student to teacher if present, following SOP *in order to* insure children are in their assigned classrooms. (HVD)

Medium (35%–60%).   Attend to requests of aged residents for assistance in seating or rising from dining table, drawing on knowledge of client assistance methods and relying on sensitivity to individual's needs *in order to* facilitate movement of residents. (TBE)

Observe and respond to gestured request from physically challenged patient for adjustment of body/bed position, drawing on knowledge of client assistance methods and relying on awareness of nonverbal communication and sensitivity to patient's needs *in order to* make the patient comfortable. (TBE)

Low (5%-30%).   Drive parents back to the Family Crisis Center as requested after they have talked to teacher, relying on courtesy and driving skills *in order to* return them to the shelter. (HVD)

Unload boxes of supplies from van, carrying boxes to the supply room; open boxes and place them on shelf, distributing requested amounts of supplies to secretary at her desk or placing supplies in cabinets at copier, relying on lifting ability and following SOP *in order to* have supplies available for staff. (HVD)

People Level 2: Exchanging Information

Definition.   Talks to, converses with, and/or signals people to convey or obtain information, or to clarify and work out details of an assignment, within the framework of well-established procedure; for example, requests clarification of a verbal signal (in person or on radio) or hand signal.

Comments.   This is the most common form of interpersonal behavior. It should be noted that a reliable vocabulary to describe skills related to this function is lacking.

Communication skills begin to show up as a requirement more frequently starting with this function. These skills include, in addition to the skills already mentioned, conversing openly—answering questions directly, straightforwardness; and speaking at level of person addressed.

Level 2: Illustrative Tasks

High (65%–90%).

Medium (35%–60%).   Meet/talk with vendors who have contacted agency or with whom there is an ongoing relationship, either in office or on site, drawing on agency requirements for vendors and available time and relying on experience *in order to* review new product, obtain pricing information, and look over quality of vendor's operation. (PUA)

Review/backtrack the inputs that produced an apparent error on printout (e.g., accounts payable, payroll), discussing matter with appropriate subordinates such as payroll clerk and program supervisor; drawing on knowledge of agency organization, programs, and financial procedures; and relying on skill in working with people *in order to* correct the error. (CAT)

Phone or write, as appropriate, accounting department, purchasing department, and/or program agency about inconsistent or incompatible commercial paper (numbers do not match, using a desk calculator; drawing on requisitions, bills, and invoices submitted for payment as necessary; and relying on experience *in order to* clear up inconsistencies and obtain legitimate paper. (APS)

Call computer center when own computer is not functioning normally (e.g., input is continuously rejected as invalid for some reason), explaining the problem, following SOP *in order to* obtain help. (APS)

Answer phones, take messages concerning absent child, transfer calls to requested person, answer general information questions about Head Start, push door opener button to allow entrance into locked building, relying on telephone skills *in order to* have site phones and entrance covered during secretary's lunch and break periods. (HVD)

Coordinate/plan logistics for training sessions, conferences, and retreats, arranging for facilities, travel, food, and overnight accommodation as necessary; ordering supplies and audiovisual equipment; confirming participation of clients by letter or phone; and relying on communication and management skills *in order to* insure a physical environment that facilitates learning. (TRS)

Low (5%–30%).   Drive to/visit stores, inquiring about needed parts and price, referring to type and quantity information supplied by secretary, giving information to the secretary for preparation of purchase order form, picking up supplies when paperwork has been processed, relying on oral communication skills, and following SOP *in order to* get parts needed to make repairs. (HVD)

(See page 124 for additional Exchanging Information tasks)

People Level 3A: Sourcing Information

Definition.   Serves as a primary and central source to external public or internal workforce of system information that is crucial in directing/routing people or workers to their destination or areas of concern and make it possible for system/organization to function. Examples: information personnel in stores and terminals; reception/routing person in large office; inventory and/or stock clerk.

Comments   The communication skills manifested at this level reflect not only sensitivity and awareness, but also technical training and experience directed at dealing with specific problems in a particular context.

Level 3S: Illustrative Tasks

High (65%–90%).   Assist parents and staff at Head Start display booth, set up at various locations (e.g., food stores, welfare offices), distribute brochures, answer questions, and tell parents about the Head Start program, drawing on knowledge of Head Start program and relying on oral communication skills *in order to* recruit children for the program. (HVD)

Answer telephone, responding with courtesy; announce agency and desire to help; listen for name of person requested by caller and in the event the caller needs help encourage him or her to express the particular need, drawing on knowledge of agency and community resources and relying on telephone skills *in order to* make appropriate connection and to refer to "First Call for Help" service if required. (SWB)

Medium (35%–60%).   Refer clients to community resources for substance abuse counseling, energy assistance, family crisis intervention, food bank, housing, and other related services designed to ease hardship, drawing on knowledge of community resources and relying on interpersonal skills and sensitivity *in order to* inform clients of social services available. (STW)

Refer clients needing direction to transitional housing program, drawing on knowledge of community resources and relying on oral communication skills *in order to* provide client time to settle on a direction and accumulate money for a security payment on an apartment. (FAM)

Present agency Board Committees (e.g., budget and finance, audit) at periodic meetings with up-to-date information on the financial status and practices associated with agency, drawing on knowledge and experience with agency programs and accounting practices and relying on presentation skills *in order to* keep them informed and obtain their recommendations or directives. (CTR)

Communicate information about agency programs or structure to the media, or to certain sections of the public, in response to calls referred by the switchboard, either having the information available or indicating that the information will be obtained and a call-back made or referral made to program or executive source, drawing on knowledge of agency programs and structure and established relations with the media and relying on oral communication skills *in order to* satisfy the information needs of the caller. (PIS)

Low (5%–30%).

(See page 124 for additional Sourcing Information tasks)

People Level 3B: Persuading

Definition.   Influences others in favor of a product, service, or point of view by talks or demonstration. Examples: demonstrates safety procedures required on a piece of equipment for compliance with new regulations; sales personnel in hardware and furniture stores, boutiques.

Comments.   Communication and interpersonal skills take on a special character for this functional level, namely, Persuading. This calls for knowing the product or subject matter well enough to be convincing as to how it will meet the client's/customer's need. It also calls for sensitivity concerning the customer's readiness threshold for receiving the message.

Level 3B: Illustrative Tasks

High (65%–90%). Defuse/dissuade individuals in threatening situations in response to calls on beeper or office from school authorities, acting as a first resort, proceeding directly to neighborhood or school, drawing on knowledge of neighborhood or experience with gang and its member, and relying on skill in establishing rapport and persuading individuals to pursue constructive directions *in order to* avoid the need to call police. (STW)

Present information on community and "First Call for Help" program needs to public bodies such as city council, state legislature, and county committees, drawing on experience with the program and statistical information and relying on presentation skills *in order to* influence public thinking and increase funding for services administered. (IRS)

Medium (35%–65%). Write content for training brochures directed at specific market for training programs, distribute brochures, and make follow-up calls, drawing on knowledge of needs of the agency and relying on written communication skills *in order to* market training programs. (TRS)

Communicate with sources of volunteers and/or work placements (e.g., volunteer centers, religious groups, universities), making phone calls and writing letters, drawing on knowledge of community, and relying on communication skills *in order to* obtain volunteers and work placements to cover the phones. (IRS)

Lobby (talk persuasively) to representatives of state, county, and municipal legislative bodies about budget cuts or program issues, promoting the agency position on these issues; drawing on knowledge of agency, its programs, and needs; and relying on presentation skills and verbal ability *in order to* convince legislators of the correctness of agency positions. (CRS)

Act as an advocate for client before a judge in court, pleading tolerance/leniency for the client and requesting he or she be assessed community service units under supervision in lieu of fine and jail sentence, drawing on a trusting relationship with client and the court, and relying on verbal skills and self-confidence *in order to* give client the opportunity to redeem him- or herself and prevent client from being labeled a criminal. (STW)

Low (5%–30%).

(See page 124 for additional Persuading tasks)

People Level 3C: Coaching

Definition.   Befriends and encourages individuals on a personal, caring basis by approximating a peer- or family-type relationship either in a one-on-one or small group situation; gives instruction, advice, and personal assistance concerning activities of daily living, the use of various institutional services, and participation in groups. Examples: gives support or encouragement to apprentice or journeyperson on unfamiliar piece of equipment; coaches students on school athletic team or sponsors new employees in a training situation.

Comments.   Coaching reflects that aspect of People skills where feelings and sensitivities count for as much or more than information. This explains why these tasks are typically given a high People orientation.

In some cases, the synonyms for coaching are less than amenable to the effect desired. This can leave no choice but to use the verb coach. In these instances, it is doubly important that the verb is used according to the definition for this function.

Level 3C: Illustrative Tasks

High (65%–90%).   Accompany client in applying for services from welfare department or other community service when the client has a reading or shyness problem, drawing on familiarity with the system and relying on reading and interpersonal skills *in order to* serve as advocate and to represent the client in obtaining services. (FAM)

Establish rapport with client on first visit and orient client as to how the agency operates, expectations of client (e.g., attendance, fees, behavior as to substance abuse and confidentiality rights), and services provided by agency; obtain demographic and other data on administrative forms, drawing on counseling and agency practice and relying on interpersonal skills, following SOP *in order to* admit client to treatment. (SAC)

Coach unemployed youth and youth at risk on how to present themselves to employers and school authorities when completing applications for employment and/or training and on the importance of self-confidence, drawing on personal experience of disability (e.g., prison record or minority status) and knowledge of opportunities existing in the community to overcome disability and relying on interpersonal skills and personal self-confidence *in order to* increase an individual's chance in obtaining a job or training. (STW)

Discuss with client and family members the need for further involvement of family members in therapeutic sessions with the client or for their participation in other counseling groups, drawing on knowledge of community resources and the counseling process and relying on oral communication skills and sensitivity *in order to* secure the continuing supportive involvement of the family for themselves and the client. (SAC)

Comfort/nurture disturbed, frightened, and crying children who have trouble separating from parents and adjusting to the school situation, drawing on training in child development and relying on experience as parents and teachers, patience, and nonverbal (body language) communication skills *in order to* quiet, calm, and reassure child to take part in activities of the classroom setting. (HST)

Medium (35%–65%).

Low (5%–30%).

(See pages 124–125 for additional Coaching tasks)

People Level 3D: Diverting

Definition.   Amuses/performs to entertain or distract individuals and/or audience or to lighten a situation. Examples: day care teaching, storytelling, street entertaining.

Comments.   For the function of Diverting, particular talents need to be manifested such as dramatizing, miming, juggling, dancing, storytelling, singing—although not necessarily on a level required for public/commercial performance.

Level 3D: Illustrative Tasks

High (65%–90%). Talk to/play games with young children in recreation area while parent(s) attend conference, drawing on knowledge of games and activities and relying on ability to establish rapport, communication skills, and special talents *in order to* divert children's attention from absence of parent(s). (TBE)

Talk/chat with client while en route to employment center or prospective employer for interview, selecting and narrating anecdotes and humorous incidents of self or others in similar situations, relying on communication and interpersonal skills and past experience *in order to* reduce nervous tension of client. (TBE)

Talk/chat with patient prior to physical therapy treatment, relating stories and/or humorous anecdotes about patients in similar situations, drawing on past experience with patients and relying on communication and interpersonal skills *in order to* reduce patient's fears and anxieties about treatment. (TBE)

Medium (35%–60%). Organize/conduct diversionary recreational activities at monthly meetings for an explorers' unit of young clients, some of whom have already had trouble with the law (intensive) and some who have not (nonintensive), drawing on knowledge of clients and community resources and relying on skill in winning confidence of clients *in order to* engage clients in constructive activities. (STW)

Entertain sick children through reading stories, playing games, or talking, drawing on knowledge of resources available locally (e.g., toys, games, children's books) and relying on communication skills and sensitivity to child's illness *in order to* provide diversion and lessen boredom due to confinement. (TBE)

Low (5%–30%).

People Level 4A: Consulting

Definition.   Serves as a source of technical knowledge and provides such knowledge as well as related ideas to define, clarify, enlarge on, or sharpen procedures, capabilities, or product specifications. Examples: informs project managers of effective and appropriate use of equipment to achieve output within constraints (time, money, etc.); presents options to solve particular problems.

Comments.   Although various degrees of subtlety are required in communication and interpersonal skills, it reaches its highest form in Consulting. Consulting frequently involves relating a body of technical data to a relatively complex, probably systematic, problem. It therefore involves understanding as much, if not more, than the client about the situation and conveying options or particular solutions in terms of their advantages and disadvantages in a manner acceptable to the client. The subtlety is called for in dealing with the interests of individual stakeholders who may prefer things as they are and are interested only in small, immediate solutions to existing problems. If they are to be won over to cooperate on more sweeping changes, the consultant must find ways to relate the changes to their needs so they are seen as advantageous to them. Subtlety, tact, patience, rapport, as well as basic honesty, are at a premium in these situations.

Level 4A: Illustrative Tasks

High (65%–90%).

Medium (35%–60%).   Present results of research to area council on priority issues such as housing and drug-related crime, including resources and funding available in the community, explaining and clarifying as necessary, drawing on knowledge of agency, community, funding sources, and projects in force and relying on presentation skills *in order to* enable council to make informed decisions on priority issues. (CRS)

Communicate with law enforcement officers, the courts, and other community agencies on the phone or in writing concerning the treatment progress of specific current clients, giving information on request or testifying in court, drawing on client files and awareness of the role of these agencies in achieving successful outcomes and ethical and confidentiality guidelines, and relying on communication and interpersonal skills *in order to* fulfill legal requirements and achieve a team approach toward helping the client. (SAC)

Discuss/consider ongoing problems and possible solutions and approaches with users (e.g., data automation or system enhancement), drawing on knowledge and experience with the processes of strategic planning and relying on problem-solving skills *in order to* decide on a particular approach suitable to the user. (DBA)

Contribute information where possible at a variety of meetings called by the director of programs, including such themes as database for computerization, energy assistance, administrative functions, and accounting procedures, drawing on experience and knowledge of special field and relying on communication skills *in order to* provide support and assist administrators. (CTD)

Low (5%–30%).   Present information about services offered by agency to a group (e.g., senior citizens, youth services, energy assistance) in response to direct requests or requests made to administrative heads of agency, by phone or letter, drawing on knowledge of the agency, its personnel and programs, assembled materials (brochures and the like), and assistance from supervisors or specialists of particular programs, and relying on communication and presentation skills *in order to* inform requesting group. (CRS)

(See pages 125–126 for additional Consulting tasks)

People Level 4B: Instructing

Definition. Teaches subject matter to others or trains others, including animals, through explanation, demonstration, and test, bringing them to a desired level of performance.

Comments. Instructing involves highly sophisticated communication and interpersonal skills in the form of presentation (including the use of audiovisual technology) and motivation skills, inspiring students to learn a particular subject matter. This includes sensitivity to and awareness of student readiness and self-esteem because learning either involves giving up something in order to make room for new information or experiencing a shift in the previous pattern of knowledge and understanding.

Level 4B: Illustrative Tasks

High (65%–90%).

Medium (35%–60%). Train program personnel in the use of a computer to enter and access data, using hands-on demonstration, including the use of a variety of function codes, accounting codes, and procedures, drawing on personal knowledge and experience with the computer system and relying on instructional skills *in order to* enable program personel to maintain financial records and to hook into master file. (ACT)

Conduct training sessions, using lesson plans previously designed, adapting the material to the learning rate of the participants and the questions that they raise, drawing on knowledge of content area, experience, and training as an instructor and relying on communication and presentation skills *in order to* facilitate the learning of the content by the participants. (TRS)

Instruct/train individuals in computer operation, in groups or one-on-one, taking them through procedures step-by-step, using prepared manual to answer questions, giving and reviewing exercises, and encouraging participants to apply training and use system as often as possible, drawing on knowledge of field and training experience and relying on communication and instructional skills *in order to* provide individuals with computer skills and knowledge. (SA)

Train youth and general assistance workers in janitorial services, demonstrating operation of scrubbing machine, mixing of cleaning solutions, and how to make minor repairs, drawing on experience and training and relying on communication and interpersonal skills *in order to* provide on-the-job training. (JAN)

Train school staff and civic officials concerned with discipline and security in the methods of identifying gang members and determining their needs and motivations, drawing on personal experience and knowledge of area and relying on presentation skills *in order to* assist participants in recognizing gang members and directing them into constructive activities. (STW)

Low (5%–30%).

(See page 126 for additional Instructing tasks)

People Level 4C: Treating

Definition.   Acts on or interacts with individuals or small groups of people or animals who need help (as in sickness) to carry out specialized therapeutic or adjustment procedures. Systematically observes results of treatment within the framework of total personal behavior because unique individual reactions to prescriptions (chemical, physical, or behavioral) may not fall within the range of expectation/prediction. Motivates, supports, and instructs individuals to accept or cooperate with therapeutic adjustment procedures when necessary.

Comments.   Treating skills probably involve the most developed form of empathizing because the learning required by the patient is frequently associated with pain. It further involves a great deal of patience and flexibility to deal with unique, individual responses to treatment. Although treatment is prescribed and more or less controlled, considering the nature of individual responses to treatment, there is space for innovativeness.

Level 4C: Illustrative Tasks

High (65%–90%).   Listen to/observe patterns of interaction among client and family members or significant others, asking family members to describe directly to client the effect of client's behavior on the family, drawing on counseling techniques, understanding of group dynamics, and observed family dynamics and relying on sensitivity, awareness, and listening skills *in order to* identify and clarify those attitudinal, communication, and behavior patterns that support or are detrimental to the client's treatment. (SAC)

Conduct/facilitate group sessions of 6 to 12 clients around topics that emerge from their interaction in the group or around specific suggested themes, encouraging clients to identify with others having similar problems and to obtain their feedback, drawing on knowlege of group dynamics and relying on group counseling techniques, sensitivity, empathy, and verbal communication skills *in order to* break down denial, build self-esteem, and practice new behaviors in a safe environment. (SAC)

Medium (35%–60%).   Query client or family in scheduled therapeutic sessions about experiences, feelings, and events during the interim between sessions, listening to and observing client and/or family member(s), confronting denial as appropriate, responding with empathy, and praising positive steps taken toward goals, drawing on therapeutic training and understanding of particular client and relying on counseling techniques, sensitivity, empathy, and verbal communication skills *in order to* carry out the therapeutic process and implement the treatment plan. (SAC)

Follow prescribed treatment plan with patient, give patient prescribed medications, assist patient as necessary, take reading of patient's tempature, blood pressure, and respiration, noting changes outside of acceptable limits, drawing on nurses' training, treatment plan, medical file, and familiarity with patient and relying on nursing skills and ability to establish rapport with patient *in order to* carry out physician's treatment plan. (NUR)

Low (5%–30%).

(See page 127 for additional Treating tasks)

People Level 5: Supervising

Definition.   Determines and/or interprets work procedure for a group of workers, assigns specific duties to them delineating prescribed and discretionary content, maintains harmonious relations among them, evaluates performance (both prescribed and discretionary) and promotes efficiency and other organizational values; makes decisions on procedural and technical levels.

Comments.   The description of tasks does not fully communicate the nuances that are associated with supervision. Supervisory behavior subsumes a wide variety of styles. Supervision, in many ways, reflects a culture. For example, authoritarian, consultative, or participative supervision reflects different cultural norms. The standards implicit in the various supervisory tasks described will vary with the norms of the cultural context in which they occur. The way in which a performance evaluation is conducted will depend on "where the supervisor is coming from" culturally and the expectations of the organization. Another important variable is the type of workers supervised, that is, their educational and cultural orientation. These orientations affect how they respond to an organization's environment, how they use their Adaptive Skills—skills concerned with management of self in relation to conformity and change, the context of jobs rather than their content.

Helpful Hints.   This function requires an almost equal measure of Data as well as People skills.

Level 5: Illustrative Tasks

High (65%–90%). Listen to staff complaints about working conditions, scheduling case loads, agency performance requirements, or interpersonal conflict, examining facts, obtaining staff suggestions for remedies, and considering options, drawing on understanding of the individual staff members and program needs and relying on interpersonal conflict resolution skills *in order to* resolve problems, boost staff morale, and maintain services. (SAC)

Conduct periodic staff meetings, sharing information about new policies, procedures, and resources; answering questions; and discussing project developments and problems, drawing on knowledge of program and relying on group dynamics skills *in order to* provide guidance and disseminate information. (IRS)

Medium (35%–60%). Talk with coordinators by phone daily, logging developments (e.g., absences, sickness, personal time off, cancelation of meetings, unusual happenings), drawing on knowledge of agency personnel policies, and relying on interpersonal skills and SOP *in order to* insure attendance, coverage in case of absences, and documentation of personnel procedures. (HSA)

Conduct performance appraisals in one-on-one meetings with individual staff, discussing performance as appropriate, drawing on agency guidelines, and relying on interpersonal skills *in order to* fulfill agency guidelines, provide feedback, and determine whether annual increase is merited. (CTD)

Evaluate performance of regular staff, selected student volunteers, and work placements periodically on basis of selection criteria, discussing evaluation on one-to-one basis and completing the necessary forms, drawing on knowledge of assignments and relying on interpersonal skills *in order to* provide feedback, acknowledgment, indication of need for further training, and fulfillment of agreement with various agencies that supply volunteers and work placements. (IRS)

Low (5%–30%). Assign staff therapists to client groups according to clients' insight into their problem and commitment to abstinence and recovery (12 distinct groups), drawing on training and program orientation and relying on experience and supervisory skills *in order to* maximize the recovery of the clients and broaden the experience of the therapists. (SAC)

(See pages 127–128 for additional Supervising tasks)

People Level 6: Negotiating

Definition. Bargains and discusses on a formal basis, as a representative of one side of a transaction, for advantages in resources, rights, privileges, and/or contractual obligations, giving and taking within the limits provided by authority or within the framework of the perceived requirements and integrity of a problem.

Comments. The interpersonal skills involved in this function require practitioners to seek advantages without feeling any compunction because opponents in the negotiation are seeking similar outcomes for themselves. However, it is believed by some that more successful and lasting outcomes are win-win rather than win-lose. Again, the Data skills are as significant as the People skills in either case.

Level 6: Illustrative Tasks

High (65%–90%).

Medium (35%–60%). Meet with financial officers, directors, contract monitors, and/or grant officers, alone or accompanied by other agency executives, regarding contract financial problems and/or misunderstandings, drawing on knowledge of particular contract or agency experience and relying on negotiating skills *in order to* clarify problems and/or obtain payments. (CTR)

Develop contracts with participating feeding sites, shelters, and pantries, specifying terms and conditions of participation in the program, conditions of storage, inventory control, and recordkeeping requirements and agency's contractual requirements and relying on negotiating skills *in order to* insure that the Soup Kitchen/Food Bank program operates in compliance with state and federal requirements. (PSC)

Contract with a variety of maintenance service and safety vendors (e.g., trash pick-up, fire inspection, elevator service) for particular services, inviting and selecting from among bids if required, drawing on specifications of services required, and relying on experience and negotiating skills *in order to* obtain services needed to maintain the integrity of the building. (CTD)

Meet/confer with legislators (local, state, federal) concerning needed or pending legislation affecting minorities and/or the poor, advising them about relevant agency experiences, understandings, and the probable effectiveness of the legislation under consideration, drawing on knowledge of agency and the community it serves or consultation with agency's executive staff and relying on interpersonal communication skills *in order to* influence legislation in favor of the needs being served by agency. (EXD)

Present annual nutrition plan to the citywide policy council, explaining information, allowing for input, and incorporating recommendations, drawing on knowledge of nutrition needs of the poor in the community and relying on presentation skills *in order to* obtain approval of plan. (HSN)

Low (5%–30%).

People Level 7: Mentoring

Definition.   Works with individuals having problems affecting their life adjustment in order to advise, counsel, and/or guide them according to legal, scientific, clinical, spiritual, and/or other professional principles. Advises clients on implications of analyses or diagnoses made of problems, courses of action open to deal with them, and merits of one strategy over another.

Comments.   As in Negotiating and Supervising, the Data skills are as significant as People skills in the practice of this function. Experience is crucial because skills must focus on individuation of therapeutic approaches. The Data skills come into focus in a diagnosis; the People skills come into focus in establishing rapport and a working relationship with the client based on confidence and trust.

Level 7: Illustrative Tasks

High (65%–90%). Counsel church members in spiritual and/or emotional distress, drawing on knowledge of pastoral care, counseling methods, and relevant spiritual doctrine and relying on communication skills and ability to relate to people from diverse backgrounds *in order to* attend to members' spiritual and emotional needs and provide spiritual guidance. (MIN)

Medium (35%–60%). Counsel client in development of coping skills, using prioritization for decision making; teaching and encouraging client to practice a variety of skills through use of such exercises as writing down unresolved painful experiences, progressive relaxation, subvocalizing (saying no repeatedly to negative thoughts), drawing on training and experience with psychodrama, role playing, and cognitive restructuring (looking at positive aspects of negative patterns) and relying on ability to establish rapport with client, empathy, and sensitivity *in order to* help client sort out problems and gain control. (SWF)

Counsel/advise client having personal and/or emotional problems, drawing on knowledge of counseling methods, theory, professional principles and guidelines, and relying on interpersonal and communication skills and ability to establish rapport *in order to* help client gain insight into personal problems and plan therapeutic action. (COP)

Conduct therapeutic interviews on a frequency schedule related to the length of time client remains in shelter (ranging from a few days to several weeks), checking off services provided on specific form, drawing on confidence gained with client assessment made in initial interview and the therapeutic technique that appears most appropriate, and relying on counseling techniques *in order to* relieve clients' pain/stress, develop a treatment plan, and enable them to take advantage of referral services. (SWF)

Discuss legal problems with client, determining legal facts of case and exploring legal options and constraints, drawing on knowledge of legal rights, practice, law, and professional guidelines and relying on interpersonal and communication skills and candor *in order to* advise client of legal options and possible courses of action. (LYR)

Low (5%–30%).

People Level 8: Leading

Definition.   Sets forth/asserts a vision that has an impact on and defines the mission, culture, and values of an organization; sets direction, time perspective, and organizational structure for achievement of goals and objectives; models behavior that inspires and motivates achievement (distinct from management).

Comments.   Leadership is unique to leaders, often associated with charisma. Leadership is often time-bound, that is, associated with an individual "seizing the moment." The particulars of individual and time make it difficult to specify particular skills. Common to many leaders is a personal epiphany, determination, and persistence of a very high order and single-mindedness. Experience does not seem to play the same role for this function as it does for those immediately preceding. Neither do Data skills.

Level 8: Illustrative Tasks

High (65%-90%). Facilitate strategic planning sessions/meetings with managers and/or employees, drawing on knowledge of strategic planning process, principles and guidelines, current corporate direction and goals, and challenges facing corporation in future and relying on communication and facilitation skills, active listening, organizational skills, and an ability to establish and maintain rapport *in order to* elicit participant's view, determine future goals, and coalesce organization around shared organizatoinal vision. (EXM)

Brainstorm/discuss problems affecting the entire agency at retreats and general conferences convened for administrative and executive staff, ask questions, probe for possible approaches to problems such as agency identity and problem definition, drawing on understanding of the needs of the agency and relying on leadership skills and ability to instill confidence and trust *in order to* establish priorities, explore feasible solutions, and develop team approaches. (EXD)

Medium (35%-60%). Develop/define organizational change strategy, with assistance and support of relevant parties as required (e.g., management departments, employee representatives), drawing on knowledge of organizational change process, organizational climate, relevant stakeholders, marketplace factors, and corporate strategy and mission and relying on patience, communication, persuasion, and presentation skills *in order to* acquire buy-in for change from relevant parties and to create an organizational change strategy. (EXM)

Low (5%-30%). Develop/create a corporate mission statement, with assistance of external/internal facilitator if necessary, drawing on knowledge of strategic management procedures and process, corporate challenges and constraints, the current organizational culture, and previous experience and relying on communication and listening skills *in order to* acquire and define a mission statement that reflects the goals and aspirations of the corporation. (EXM)

Additional Illustrative Tasks: People Functions

Level 2: Exchanging Information

Low. Visit sites of Head Start programs, talk to appropriate personnel as required, examine attendance records, do head counts, and verify the acquisition of equipment (capital expenditures), drawing on agency guidelines and budgets and relying on experience *in order to* insure delegate agencies are performing in accordance with regulations. (PRA)

Review new and revised software, such as operating systems, word processing, and networking programs, routinely received from computer vendors; read through accompanying questionnnaires, concerned with their practicality, obtaining clarification from vendor by phone as necessary, drawing on experience with existing software and met and unmet needs *in order to* decide whether to install new software. (SYA)

Level 3A: Sourcing Information

Medium. Inform employees, their supervisors, delegate agencies, and outside agencies (e.g., loan companies, welfare department) about payroll and/or benefits, accessing the computer for information, drawing on knowledge of agency personnel policies, and relying on communication skills *in order to* provide information reqested. (PSS)

Level 3B: Pursuading

Medium. Talk to/discuss with parents their involvement in the Head Start program, encouraging participation in their children's education, taking into account their availability as well as classroom needs, drawing on knowledge of Head Start program, and relying on communication and interpersonal skills *in order to* recruit volunteers for classrooms. (HSN)

Level 3C: Coaching

High. Model eating behavior and manners for children; serve family-style breakfast; eat with children; encourage children to serve themselves as food is passed from one to the other; commend proper eating manners and sanitary behavior in handling utensils, silverware, and food; describe nutritional value of food in language children can understand; observe and listen to children's comments about their experiences at home and at play, drawing on training and relying on sensitivity to each child's moods *in order to* teach appropriate eating habits and cooperative behaviors. (HST)

Participate/interact with clients in group attending such special events as professional ball games, bowling, training classes, and picnics, modeling and monitoring positive social behaviors, drawing on knowledge and interests of clients, and relying on awareness of group interactions *in order to* promote relationship with clients and share a reward for cooperation in program(s). (STW)

Counsel one-on-one with each client who is registered for various services in Youth Development Plan program, discussing activity in school, job, and family situations, drawing on understanding of the degree of at-risk seriousness of client's situation, and relying on interpersonal and communication skills *in order to* monitor progress and establish the need for additional or augmented services. (STW)

Level 4A: Consulting

Medium. Listen to presentations made by staff members and graduate and undergraduate student interns of their current cases, read and review their documentation, discuss with them the rationale of their proposed and utilized interventions, drawing on personal clinical training and role as supervisor of center and relying on experience and interpersonal skills *in order to* assess information-gathering process and make recommendations concerning diagnostic thinking, treatment planning, and use and effectiveness of treatment interventions. (SAC)

Obtain data about family history, presenting problem and client goals, discussing with client the treatment plan to be followed, which could include a combination of individual, group, and family therapy sessions and substance abuse group education, drawing on the policies of the agency and background training in counseling techniques and relying on communication skills *in order to* prepare clients for the treatment process in which they will be involved. (SAC)

Review/monitor the selection process, answering questions of hiring supervisor, advising on interviewing procedures, reviewing documentation provided by supervisors in support of their recommendation for hire, comparing applicant to current staff in similar positions for equity in salary requested, drawing on knowledge of agency policies and procedures, relevant labor laws/regulations, internal managerial styles and preferences, and relying on verbal and written communication skills *in order to* insure vacancies are filled with qualified applicants. (PSU)

Low. Conduct a needs assessment for a specific training program or for an agencywide training plan, either interviewing staff and supervisors, in group or individual sessions, or distributing questionnaires to relevant staff, drawing on experience in conducting needs assessments and knowledge of particular group and relying on analytical skills *in order to* generate the content base for a specific training curriculum or an agencywide training plan. (TRS)

Level 4B: Instructing

Medium. Oversee and evaluate student work on curriculum outline sheets that lay out developmental exercises for each subject, walking around the class and checking each student's work, stopping activity when a common problem arises for class discussion, drawing on lesson plans and relying on instructional skills *in order to* observe and check each student's progress. (GED)

Train accounting staff in accounting methodology appropriate to the agency, using classroom sessions, drawing on prepared lesson plans, audiovisual presentations, specially prepared exercises designed to reinforce learning, knowledge of training techniques and relying on instructional skills *in order to* prepare accountants to undertake responsibilities and insure uniform processing of data. (CAT)

Oversee/guide children aged 3 to 5 in clean up and wash up, including disposing of dishes, washing space at table, washing hands and face, brushing teeth, and personal toileting, with assistance as necessary, drawing on knowledge and understanding of early child development and relying on skill in guiding young children *in order to* model and teach cleanliness, responsibility, and personal hygiene. (HST)

Level 4C: Treating

Medium.   Describe/demonstrate prescribed exercises to patient with "severe low back condition," guide and encourage patient in performing exercises, observing and judging patient's movement in relation to norms and indications of pain, drawing on physical therapy training, prescribed treatment plan, and familiarity with patient and relying on interpersonal skills, ability to establish rapport with patient, and awareness of patient's tolerance of pain *in order to* relieve pain, increase relaxation, and restore mobility. (PHT)

Level 5: Supervising

Medium.   Observe teaching staff in classroom situations, noting teacher/assistant relationship, teacher/child interaction, unrest in classroom and evaluating the effectiveness of the teaching team, drawing on observations, teaching criteria, and knowledge of child development and relying on observation and writing skills *in order to* provide education supervisor with written information about teaching staff at site. (HSN)

Oversee outreach workers, giving and monitoring assignments, assisting them in initiating assignments, giving training on the job in the community, drawing on knowledge and experience as an outreach worker, and relying on supervisory and interpersonal skills *in order to* conduct the activities of the outreach program. (STW)

Low.   Oversee the preparation of financial reports, or prepare them using computer, in response to management requirments and/or special requirements (e.g., of funding agency, executives, program directors), providing technical assistance to the staff in the preparation of data, drawing on knowledge of accounting and computer software, and relying on attention to detail *in order to* meet requirements and provide general management information. (CTR)

Dispatch crew of laborers to monitor the fair, secure fair, and systematically unload and distribute commodities to eligible households, giving precise instructions about the type of food, the size of crowds, and scheduling requirements, relying on experience *in order to* prevent theft, minimize crowding, and insure order is maintained and undistributed food returned to warehouse. (PSC)

WORKER INSTRUCTIONS SCALE

The premise of this scale is based on the fact that everything workers do on the job involves an instruction, either given by management or by the worker to him- or herself. The instruction has two elements: *prescription and discretion*. The *prescribed* part of an instruction contains what is known and is generally proceduralized and, if at all possible, standardized. It appears as specifications, work orders, blueprints, exploded drawings, plans and assignments. A worker will receive them at the start of a job of work, as an integral part of training, or both.

The *discretionary* part of instructions, the part left to the worker's judgment, is typically not specified. However, the greater the duration of job training, for example, college and beyond, the more the worker is expected to use discretion and depend on guidelines rather than specific proceduralized instructions. This is generally referred to as using one's initiative, being a self-starter, and the like.

Assembly-line work and work involved with tending highly automated equipment is highly prescribed work leaving little to the judgment of the worker. Professional work is highly discretionary, although there are specified aspects to this work as well, more where there is hardware involved and less where the work deals with people and with the arts. Together, the prescribed and discretionary instructions can be considered to be 100% of the instructions a worker must follow. In this context, it is possible to say for a particular job that 75% of the instructions are prescribed and therefore 25% discretionary, or vice versa.

It is useful to think of this conceptualization of worker instructions in connection with understanding the meaning of *experience*. In the early stages of a job or career, an individual needs to learn that which is prescribed and already standardized. As time goes on the worker inevitably encounters situations that are not prescribed and therefore require discretion, either for working out personal solutions or seeking help. Where the work is proceduralized, this is indicated in task statements by the phrase "following SOP (standing operating procedures)". Where a significant amount of discretion is required, this is indicated by "relying on experience." It is possible for both to occur in the same task statement, reflecting the fact that there is a mixture of specification and discretion involved.

Worker Instructions Benchmarks

Level 1

Definition. Inputs, outputs, tools, equipment, and procedures are all specified. Almost everything the worker needs to know is contained in the assignment. The worker usually turns out a specified amount of work or a standard number of units per hour or day.

Level 1: Illustrative Tasks

Separate the three copies of a computer printed check for signatures and mailing, compare the commercial paper to one copy as a final check for possible corrections, forward original copy for signature, and place the third copy in book of issued checks, following SOP *in order to* effect payments and maintain record of payments made. (APS)

Mix cleaning solution(s) in bucket, drawing on knowledge of cleaning agents and methods, following SOP *in order to* clean floors. (JAN)

Sort/distribute incoming mail, drawing on familiarity with established distribution route within department, following SOP *in order to* have mail reach appropriate person. (JAN)

Retrieve purchase orders produced by Data Department, sort for amount, giving special attention to orders that require dual signatures, following SOP *in order to* sign off on purchase orders. (PUA)

Remove filter from window air conditioner, clean with mild detergent, replace with new filter if necessary, and vacuum inside the housing of the conditioner, following SOP *in order to* maintain upkeep of air conditioners. (JAN)

Distribute four copies of purchase orders by mail and internal messenger to vendors, accounting, and originating project, following SOP *in order to* activate the purchase and keep the systems informed. (PUA)

Fit lock assembly over predrilled holes and screw into door and jamb, following SOP *in order to* complete the lock installation. (HST)

Punch collated materials with a three-hole punch when specified, following SOP *in order to* ready paper for insertion into three-ring binders. (SWB)

Turn/open gate valves on boiler to release water, sediments, and steam at water column at front of boiler daily for 3 seconds and at back of boiler 3 times weekly for 10 seconds, drawing on knowledge and experience with boiler system, following SOP *in order to* clear out sediments from boiler. (JAN)

Worker Instructions Level 2

Definition.   Inputs, outputs, tools, and equipment are all specified, but the worker has some leeway in the procedures and methods used to get the job done. Almost all the information needed is in the assignment instructions. Production is measured on a daily or weekly basis.

Level 2: Illustrative Tasks

Review/scan room set-up with reference to the day's lesson plan for furniture arrangement, materials, and supplies, removing chairs from tables and wiping tables down *in order to* insure that equipment and materials are available for day's planned activities. (HST)

Move furniture into configurations appropriate for type of meeting (e.g., lecture, seminar), following oral instructions *in order to* have room set up. (JAN)

Assist children in getting out of van, walk them to their classroom, give the teacher a copy of any new student forms, and introduce parent(s) of new student to teacher if present, following SOP *in order to* insure children are in their assigned classrooms. (HVD)

Inventory classroom supplies and materials using special inventory forms; order new materials as needed for upcoming semester; clean materials before packing, labeling major equipment and furniture; and store materials over school breaks, following SOP *in order to* have materials and supplies available for following school year. (HST)

Drive van to downtown offices when directed by site supervisors or agency transportation coordinator, pick up mail or previously ordered supplies and completed duplication orders, load them onto the van, and drop them off at the appropriate sites, drawing on knowledge of location of agency administrative services and relying on driving and lifting ability *in order to* insure sites receive their requested materials. (HVD)

Post accounting transactions into accounting system daily, drawing on knowledge of agency system, computer software, and relying on attention to detail *in order to* update system and keep information current. (CAT)

Worker Instructions Level 3

Definition.   Inputs and outputs are specified, but the worker has considerable freedom as to procedure and timing, including the use of tools and/or equipment. The worker may have to refer to several standard sources for information (handbooks, catalogs, wall charts). Time to complete a particular product or service is specified, but this varies up to several hours.

Level 3: Illustrative Tasks

Review paperwork for projects being audited, such as purchase requisitions, payment authorizations, check requests, consultant contracts and payments, travel reimbursements; sign off and forward for disposition, following agency accounting practices *in order to* approve or reject disbursements. (ACT)

Compile/examine composite printouts of data on particular programs (e.g., child care, substance abuse, aid to the elderly) for currency and accuracy, comparing printout with commercial paper (e.g., invoices, accounts payable), entering data on formats provided or prepared within agency *in order to* provide financial reports required by granting agencies. (ACT)

Repair/replace broken equipment such as door handles, locks, splintered wooden toys, and knocking radiators, or assemble new prefabricated equipment upon request from site supervisor, drawing on knowledge of general repair and relying on skill in handling tools *in order to* insure equipment at sites is in working order. (HVD)

Set up/maintain file for each client consisting of the forms completed on intake, progress notes after each individual or family session, notes received from group facilitator, and correspondence received from referral agencies and originating therapist, relying on self-management and clericial skills *in order to* meet requirements of contract supporting the agency, which includes legal and ethical requirements of the counseling profession. (SAC)

Review computer printouts showing state taxes deducted from individual salaries for all agency and delegate agencies within a tax payment period, compare it with checks for taxes accumulated and issued by accounts payable, and complete and mail checks and state tax forms by deadline, drawing on knowledge of tax regulations and following SOP *in order to* insure that taxes are paid and penalties avoided. (PSS)

Schedule/evaluate monthly fire drills and intermittent tornado drills for Head Start sites; provide dates and times to maintenance staff and teaching staff; conduct on-site evaluations including bathroom, classroom, and office checks; and monitor time and attendance factors, drawing on knowledge of safety procedures, relying on attention to detail and observation skills, and following SOP *in order to* insure that staff and children are prepared for disaster and sites comply with state licensing regulations. (HSN)

(See page 146 for additional Level 3 tasks)

Worker Instructions Level 4

Definition.   Output (product or service) is specified in the assignment, which may be in the form of a memorandum or of a schematic (sketch or blueprint). The worker must work out own way of getting the job done, including selection and use of tools and/or equipment, sequence of operations (tasks), and obtaining important information (handbooks, etc.). Worker may either do the work or set up standards and procedures for others to do it.

Comments.   The work of most journeypersons tends to be organized around this level of instructions.

Level 4: Illustrative Tasks

Prepare/write article for newsletter, home visit report, parent–teacher conference, and progress report on child, drawing on professional training and special workshop education, relying on writing skills, and following SOP *in order to* promote communication with parents about their children and parent involvement with Head Start activity. (HST)

Inspect client's home, usually in response to a call immediately following a break-in; install locks on front and rear doors as necessary; check residence for other needs such as barring windows, replacing window panes, installing window pins; and measure for materials, drawing on experience and relying on ability to use measuring tools *in order to* prepare a work order for completion at a later date. (HST)

Assign and delegate work assignments to staff members consistent with level of training and ability; coach and train staff member on the job; approve time cards, vacation, and personal time; and carry out performance appraisal annually *in order to* get work out and encourage and support staff. (APS)

Inform/describe to auditors (e.g., outside auditor, funding source) the various formats and data sources, files, printouts, relevant to agency accounting system, responding to their inquiries as requested, drawing on knowledge of and experience with agency system and agency accounting practices, and relying on interpersonal skills *in order to* assist auditors. (ACT)

Train program personnel in the use of a computer to enter and access data, using hands-on demonstration, including the use of a variety of function codes, accounting codes, and procedures, drawing on personal knowledge and experience with the computer system and relying on instructional skills *in order to* enable program personnel to maintain financial records and to access master file. (ACT)

Delegate to staff or undertake on own the gathering of data relevant to an upcoming meeting or written appeal concerning a contract problem or misunderstanding, drawing on knowledge of particular issue/contract and agency operations, and relying on personal judgment *in order to* be prepared to explain or defend agency position. (CTR)

Share/communicate and absorb information and experience presented during staff and seminar meetings *in order to* stay informed about what is going on in agency and acquire new skills and knowledge. (PSS)

(See pages 146–147 for additional Level 4 tasks)

Worker Instructions Level 5

Definition.   Same as Level 4, but in addition the workers are expected to know and employ theory so they understand the whys and wherefores of the various options that are available for dealing with a problem and can independently select from among them. Workers may have to do some reading in the professional and/or trade literature in order to gain this understanding and/or seek assistance from a technical "expert."

Comments.   The work of most entering professionals tends to assume the ability to follow this level of instructions.

Level 5: Illustrative Tasks

Meet with department head and listen to statement of need and required output (e.g., accounting), review the existing computer files that will be an input source, write an appropriate program that processes the data as requested, test the program on a sample problem, review results with end user, modify as necessary, drawing on knowledge of content area and relying on programming experience and problem-solving skills *in order to* prepare a program that meets specifications of end user. (SYA)

Present on-the-job, hands-on orientation to program directors and supervisors, using the existing policies and procedures on purchasing as a point of departure, describing and explaining the highlights of procedures such as forms to be completed, channels to be followed, and limitations to be observed, relying on communication skills *in order to* inform those with purchasing authority of correct procedures. (PUA)

Attend special courses dealing with purchasing at university and/or professional organization, drawing on personal needs or knowledge and relying on experience, initiative, and awareness of the need of the agency to attain a high degree of effectiveness *in order to* keep up to date, enhance knowledge of field, and acquire special skills. (PUA)

Estimate/formulate annual budgets for each of the grant areas, using a computer, making tradeoffs as necessary to stay within the guidelines for the specified programs, drawing on anticipated costs and income, projected salary increases, vendor costs, utilities, insurance, and the ceiling placed on the probable amount to be granted, and relying on analytical skills *in order to* develop the optimum spending plan for the year. (CTD)

Review vendors' newly developed software that appears practical for agency operations, requesting copies for tryout, testing, and evaluation of problems that agency is experiencing (e.g., archiving, tutoring operators for word processing), drawing on knowledge of agency needs and relying on experience with computer operations and analytical skills *in order to* decide whether to requisition new programs. (SYA)

Develop training needs questionnaire for distribution to agency staff using existing questionnaires, adapting them to particular considerations such as how the questionnaire will be understood by respondents and the manner in which the data will be compiled, drawing on knowledge of agency and relying on training experience *in order to* generate data for an agency-wide training plan. (TRS)

(See page 147 for additional Level 5 tasks)

Worker Instructions Level 6

Definition. Various possible outputs are described that can meet stated technical or administrative needs. The worker must investigate the various possible outputs and evaluate them in regard to performance characteristics and input demands. This usually requires creative use of theory well beyond referring to standard sources. There is no specification of inputs, methods, sequences, sources, or the like.

Comments. The work of contractors, especially where estimating is involved and a standardized solution is not available, tends to involve this level of instruction.

Level 6: Illustrative Tasks

Review applications submitted through the Human Resources Development Office for a staff vacancy, drawing on knowledge of position and agency criteria, following SOP *in order to* select candidates to be interviewed for vacancy and to notify Human Resources Development Office of need to check references. (CAT)

Read/review articles, reports, papers, and statistical data relevant to agency, whether referred to by staff or discovered on own, taking notes as necessary, drawing on personal background and understanding, and relying on reading comprehension *in order to* enhance understanding, discover relationships, and develop materials that contribute to vision and/or provide information for speeches, presentations, or discussions with staff. (EXD)

Read/review/comment on requests for proposals (RFPs) and associated budgets, particularly objectives and scope of work, evaluating them in terms of agency's capabilities and facilities, drawing on knowledge and understanding of agency and relying on reading and conceptual skills *in order to* insure the proposals are consistent with agency vision and its capacity to deliver a result. (EXD)

Discuss with coordinators the training needs indicated in their individual task banks, reviewing with them the specifics implicit in their expressed needs and the circumstances in which the training might best occur (e.g., on-the-job vs. formal class, visiting specialist), drawing on the needs analysis, federal guidelines, and consultation with deputy director and relying on analytical and interpersonal skills *in order to* arrive at curricular and training decisions. (HSA)

Review/examine database packages on the market (e.g., Paradox, Oracle) that are capable of providing the increased data processing capacity required by agency's developing needs (e.g., the need to cross-reference the clients' database for various services they are receiving in different agency programs), drawing on understanding of current agency system, attendance at seminars, and comments of visiting current users and relying on experience *in order to* recommend a possible changeover. (SYA)

Discuss with clients their perception of training needs (e.g.,content, time, money, type of, and number of participants, methods), indicating various approaches and possibilities including customized needs assessment, drawing on knowledge of the agency, and relying on training experience and interpersonal skills *in order to* determine what will be delivered and the cost for such services incorporated in a letter of agreement by the agency. (TRS)

(See pages 147–148 for additional Level 6 tasks)

Worker Instructions Level 7

Definition.   There is some question as to what the need or problem really is or what directions should be pursued in dealing with it. In order to define the problem, to control and explore the behavior of the variables, and to formulate possible outputs and their performance characteristics, the worker must consult largely unspecified sources of information and devise investigations, surveys, or data analysis studies (strategies).

Comments.   This level of instruction typically characterizes scientific research and independent artistic endeavor. It relates to amorphous situations that sometimes lead to creative solutions.

Level 7: Illustrative Tasks

Meet with client in scheduled therapeutic sessions—individual or family—inquiring about experiences, feelings, and events during the interim between sessions; listening to and observing client and/or family member(s); confronting denial as appropriate; responding with empathy; and praising positive steps taken toward goals, drawing on therapeutic training and understanding of particular client and relying on counselling techniques, sensitivity, empathy, and verbal communication skills *in order to* carry out the therapeutic process and to implement the treatment plan. (SAC)

Consult/define organization development issues in response to requests from managers and program administrators, meeting with them in brainstorming sessions (e.g., 5-year strategic plan), drawing on knowledge of organization development, and relying on facilitative skills and experience in agency *in order to* define and clarify the problem. (TRS)

Conceive/intuit/explore relationships among selected theories and techniques from outside social work discipline and integrate them with accepted social work practice, relying on research and writing skills and previous social work experience *in order to* develop/test a new problem-solving process for multiproblem family. (TBE)

Conceive/create an original hypothesis about the nature of social-psychological problems of an ethnic or socioeconomic group, drawing on an understanding of theory and conceptual models and relying on analytical and writing skills *in order to* explain factors and phenomena previously unrecognized or unaccounted for. (TBE)

Worker Instructions Level 8

Definition.   Information and/or direction comes to the worker in terms of needs (tactical, organizational, strategic, financial). Workers must call for staff reports and recommendations concerning methods of dealing with them. They coordinate both organizational and technical data in order to make decisions and determinations regarding courses of action (outputs) for major sections (divisions, groups) of the organization.

Comments.   This level of instruction tends to describe how it is for top executives, in short, top-level responsibility for executing plans, programs, missions.

Level 8: Illustrative Tasks

Review/identify needs for additional community services and programs based on a variety of inputs (e.g., staff working in area, tenants), drawing on knowledge of center facilities and possible alliances with other agencies and available funding and relying on personal judgment and conceptualization skills *in order to* explore the feasibility of program expansion or development of a new program. (CTD)

Explore with heads of other community agencies (e.g., schools, welfare, employment) areas of mutual interest affecting the poor and minorities and considering projects warranting mutual cooperation and possible shared funding (e.g., providing services to "latch key" children), drawing on knowledge of agency and its potential, community needs and understanding of functions performed by the other agencies and relying on interpersonal and communication skills *in order to* develop specific cooperative programs and/or support for ongoing programs. (EXD)

Brainstorm/discuss problems affecting the entire agency at retreats and general conferences convened for administrative and executive staff, ask questions, probe for possible approaches to problems such as agency identity and problem definition, drawing on understanding of the needs of the agency and relying on leadership skills and ability to instill confidence and trust *in order to* establish priorities, explore feasible solutions, and develop team approaches. (EXD)

Facilitate strategic planning sessions/meetings with managers and/or employees, drawing on knowledge of strategic planning process, principles, and guidelines, current corporate direction and goals, and challenges facing corporation in the future and relying on communication and facilitation skills, active listening, organizational skills, and an ability to establish and maintain rapport *in order to* elicit participants' views, determine future goals, and coalesce organization around shared organizational vision. (EXM)

Develop/define organizational change strategy with assistance and support of relevant parties as required (e.g., management departments, employee representatives), drawing on knowledge of organizational change process, organizational climate, relevant stakeholders, marketplace factors, and corporate strategy and mission and relying on patience, communication, persuasion, and presentation skills *in order to* acquire buy-in for change from relevant parties and create an organizational change strategy. (EXM)

(See page 148 for additional Level 8 tasks)

Additional Illustrative Tasks: Worker Instructions

Level 3

Model eating behavior and manners for children; serve family-style breakfast; eat with children; encourage children to serve themselves as food is passed from one to the other; commend proper eating manners and sanitary behavior in handling utensils, silverware, and food; describe nutritional value of food in language children can understand; observe and listen to children's comments about their experiences at home and at play, drawing on training and relying on sensitivity to each child's moods *in order to* teach appropriate eating habits and cooperative behaviors. (HST)

Review physical nutrition assessment form of each child completed by parent and doctor, noting poor eating habits, blood pressure, and blood test results (e.g., high lead, low hematocrit or hemoglobin), drawing on knowledge of interpreting blood tests and level of nutrition and relying on attention to detail *in order to* assess the nutritional status of each child. (HSN)

Prepare/write and issue media notices monthly and every three months to community at large, notifying them of scheduled distributions, drawing on program schedules and requirements and relying on writing skills *in order to* inform the public of food distribution schedule. (PSC)

Check equipment (e.g, file cabinets, desks, chairs) for state of usefulness and need for additional equipment, completing purchase requisitions when necessary, drawing on furnishing standards in regulations, relying on observation skills, and following SOP *in order to* insure that site is furnished and safe. (HSN)

Level 4

Prepare/decorate classroom setting with colored construction paper, picture cutouts, corrugated paper, thematic materials relating to specified learning areas (e.g., nutrition, science, health, emergency procedures, music, multiculture); post library and parent news on bulletin boards, drawing on federal guidelines and aesthetic interests and relying on personal initiative and decorative ability *in order to* design a colorful, stimulating, well-balanced environment. (HST)

Inspect delegate agency sites according to a schedule set up by Head Start Administrator; talk with appropriate staff (e.g., cook, program assistant, teacher); review agency nutrition plan, lesson plans, menus, records, nutrition assessments for nutritional content; inspect kitchens for sanitation practices; observe the atmosphere of the eating experience (family-style eating, socialization); note use of appropriate-sized utensils, chairs, and tables, drawing on knowledge of Head Start guidelines and relying on communication and observation skills *in order to* insure that guidelines are being followed. (HSN)

Interview qualified candidates jointly with deputy director, using a list submitted by HRD for a particular vacancy, drawing on knowledge of position and prepared screening questions and relying on interpersonal skills *in order to* select the top three for recommendation to City Personnel Committee. (HSA)

Level 5

Write nutrition information packets/booklets, illustrate concepts using everyday terminology, drawing on knowledge of nutrition, technical information, and needs of parents and relying on writing skills and ability to adapt materials to specific target populations *in order to* provide parents with tools for understanding nutritional concepts. (HSN)

Interview staff members using FJA technique, describe the method to the individual, proceed systematically drawing on FJA training and the responses to five basic questions, relying on listening and writing skills *in order to* organize participants' input into standard FJA task structure and produce task statements. (TRS)

Prepare and conduct a citywide orientation for new staff in the delegate agency on the goals, objectives, mission, structure, and federal requirements of the Head Start program, drawing on knowledge of program and relying on experience and presentation skills *in order to* enable everyone in the Head Start program to see the "big picture" and operate according to the same basic philosophy. (HSA)

Prepare/write lesson plans once a week for entire following week, developing curriculum items that will be covered in class, specifying exercises/activities to be accomplished, drawing on textbook materials and teacher training and relying on experience and instructional skills *in order to* outline classwork for students for entire week. (GED)

Level 6

Counsel client in development of coping skills, using prioritization for decision making, teaching, and encouraging client to practice a variety of skills through use of such exercises as writing down unresolved painful experiences, progressive relaxation, subvocalizing (saying no repeatedly to negative thoughts), drawing on training and experience with psychodrama, role playing, and cognitive restructuring (looking at positive aspects of negative patterns) and relying on ability to establish rapport with client, empathy, and sensitivity *in order to* help clients sort out their problems and gain control. (SWF)

Discuss/explore individuallly with staff members, work-related problems, or problems dealing with their "future" in the agency, listen to their statement of the problem; inquire about the actions and outcomes they have undertaken on their own, relying on experience and communication and interpersonal skills *in order to* arrive at a mutually acceptable course of action. (EXD)

Level 8

Develop/create a corporate mission statement, with assistance of external/internal facilitator if necessary, drawing on knowledge of strategic management procedures and process, corporate challenges and constraints, the current organizational culture, and previous experience and relying on communication and listening skills *in order to* acquire and define a mission statement that reflects the goals and aspirations of the corporation. (EXM)

REASONING DEVELOPMENT SCALE

The Reasoning Development Scale is concerned with knowledge and ability to deal with theory versus practice, abstract versus concrete, and many versus few variables.

Reasoning Development Benchmarks

Level 1

Definition. Have the common-sense understanding to carry out simple one- or two-step instructions in the context of highly standardized situations.

Recognizes unacceptable variations from the standard and takes emergency action to reject inputs or stop operations.

Level 1: Illustrative Tasks

Sort/distribute incoming mail, drawing on familiarity with established distribution route within department, following SOP *in order to* have mail reach appropriate person. (APS)

Match approved requisition with numbers on computer-generated purchase order, relying on attention to detail and following agency accounting procedure *in order to* insure that they are accurate and exact. (APS)

Phone director of the Family Crisis Center daily, asking if there will be any children attending either the morning or afternoon Head Start session, relying on courtesy skills and following SOP *in order to* determine if a pick up is necessary and insure that new children that day will be accompanied by parent. (HVD)

Fit lock assembly over predrilled holes and screw into door and jamb, following SOP *in order to* complete the lock installation. (HST)

Check boiler water level daily according to specifications, adding water if low *in order to* insure boiler is operating properly. (JAN)

Type labels for individual folders for incoming material, relying on clerical skills and following SOP *in order to* prepare files for new material. (SWB)

Punch collated materials with a three-hole punch when specified, following SOP *in order to* ready paper for insertion into three-ring binders. (SWB)

Open gate valve on water column of boiler system once every three years, drawing on SOP *in order to* to drain and clean boiler system, and insure proper maintenance. (JAN)

Enter/key-in gross amounts granted by funding sources into computerized accounting system when funds are initially made available, drawing on agency accounting practices and relying on computer skills *in order to* record a receivable. (ACT)

Reasoning Development Level 2

Definition.   Have the common-sense understanding to carry out detailed but uninvolved instructions where the work involves a few concrete/specific variables in or from standard/typical situations.

Level 2: Illustrative Tasks

Drive automatic shift van between the Community Center and the Family Crisis Shelter; wait for staff and parents to bring the children to the van, going into the center to inform receptionist that the Head Start Van has arrived for pick-up as necessary; assist the children into the van; buckle their seat belts; lock the doors; checks off names on attendance sheet, adding names and starting dates of new students as appropriate and following SOP *in order to* safely transport children to the Head Start site from the Family Crisis Center. (HVD)

Seal gym floor from moisture, pour sealer solvent solution into bucket in which two regular-size bath towels have been immersed, remove a towel and wrap around mop, mop floor following length of floor grain with wrapped mop, redip and alternate towels, and overlap areas mopped until entire floor is treated with sealer solvent solution, drawing on cleaning techniques and SOP *in order to* prepare gym floor for polishing. (JAN)

Arrange tables and chairs as requested by Community Center coordinator, make coffee, set up sign on desk with sign-in sheets, and place signs on appropriate tables, drawing on directions of coordinator and following SOP *in order to* have room ready for meetings. (HVD)

Watch/monitor boiler central panel, which indicates outside temperature and water temperature inside the boiler, adjusting thermal control for water temperature when necessary, drawing on knowledge of gas-operated boiler system, and following SOP *in order to* maintain heat in the building. (JAN)

Answer telephone, responding with courtesy; announce agency and desire to help; listen for name of person requested by caller; and in the event the caller needs help encourage him or her to express a particular need, drawing on knowledge of agency and community resources and relying on telephone skills *in order to* make appropriate connection and to refer to "First Call for Help" service if required. (SWB)

Remove filter from window air conditioner, clean with mild detergent, replace with new filter if necessary, and vacuum inside the housing of the conditioner, following SOP *in order to* maintain upkeep of air conditioners. (JAN)

Complete a receiving report when requisitioned material arrives, note requested information such as quantity and condition, attach report to invoice, and forward it to accounts payable, following SOP *in order to* have supplies/materials paid for. (SWB)

(See page 162 for additional Level 2 tasks)

Reasoning Development Level 3

Definition. Have the common-sense understanding to carry out instruction where the work involves several concrete/specific variables in or from standard/typical situations.

Level 3: Illustrative Tasks

Phone or write, as appropriate, accounting department, purchasing department, and/or program agency about inconsistent or incompatible commercial paper (numbers do not match), using a desk calculator, drawing on requisitions, bills, and invoices submitted for payment as necessary and relying on experience *in order to* clear up inconsistencies and obtain legitimate paper. (APS)

Alert/notify computer users to log off the computer and key in entry codes for the computer to accept the journal, accounts payable, and payroll entries made since the previous update, drawing on agency accounting practices and following SOP *in order to* update the master file. (ACT)

Vacuum/mop carpeted areas and floors, using vacuum cleaner and wet/dry mop, wiping desks, tables, counters, blackboards, front door windows, and walls as needed, and emptying waste baskets and ash trays into trash containers, following SOP *in order to* clean rooms in building on a daily basis. (JAN)

Prepare/fill out report form for items requisitioned that have a useful life of more than 1 year and cost over $300 (fixed assests), key information into computer, drawing on agency policy to account for fixed assets and following SOP *in order to* inform accounting and fulfill requirements for designation and tracking of such assets. (PUA)

Model eating behavior and manners for children; serve family-style breakfast; eat with children; encourage children to serve themselves as food is passed from one to the other; commend proper eating manners and sanitary behavior in handling utensils, silverware, and food; describe nutritional value of food in language children can understand; observe and listen to children's comments about their experiences at home and at play, drawing on training and relying on sensitivity to each child's moods *in order to* teach appropriate eating habits and cooperative behaviors. (HST)

Repair/replace broken equipment such as door handles, locks, splintered wooden toys, and knocking radiators, or assemble new prefabricated equipment upon request from site supervisor, drawing on knowledge of general repair and relying on skill in handling tools *in order to* insure equipment at sites is in working order. (HVD)

Fill out/check off various forms such as field trip, maintenance checklist, food service checklist, attendance records, and state public school referrals, relying on experience and following agency procedures *in order to* document events for administrative purposes. (HST)

(See page 162 for additional Level 3 tasks)

Reasoning Development Level 4

Definition.   Have knowledge of a system of interrelated procedures, such as bookkeeping, internal combustion engines, electric wiring systems, nursing, farm management, ship sailing, or machining, and the ability to access optional solutions to ordinary problems.

Applies principles to solve practical everyday problems and deal with a variety of concrete variables in situations where only limited standardization exists.

Interprets a variety of instructions furnished in written, oral, diagrammatic, or schedule form.

Level 4: Illustrative Tasks

Review purchase requisition of services and goods for description and dollar amount, adherence to funding source procurement and agency approval policies, phoning calls to vendors for current information and price as necessary, drawing on catalog resources, agency policies, and procedures and relying on attention to detail *in order to* insure accuracy and legitimacy of purchase requisition and approve it for entry into computer. (PUA)

Train youth and general assistance workers in janitorial services, demonstrating operation of scrubbing machine, mixing of cleaning solutions, and how to make minor repairs, drawing on experience and training and relying on communication and interpersonal skills *in order to* provide on-the-job training. (JAN)

Inspect client's home, usually in response to a call immediately following a break-in; install locks on front and rear doors as necessary; check residence for other needs such as barring windows, replacing window panes, installing window pins; and measure for materials, drawing on experience and relying on ability to use measuring tools *in order to* prepare a work order for completion at a later date. (HST)

Review expenditures such as invoices, vouchers, and receiving reports, either periodically or when problems occur, using computer to access account information and files if original documents need to be checked, drawing on knowledge of program and relying on own initiative and experience *in order to* insure accuracy of data and conformity with the conditions of grant. (ACT)

Present on-the-job, hands-on orientation to program directors and supervisors, using the existing policies and procedures on purchasing as a point of departure; describing and explaining the highlights of procedures such as forms to be completed, channels to be followed, and limitations to be observed, relying on communication skills *in order to* inform those with purchasing authority of correct procedures. (PUA)

Respond to phone calls and personal visits by vendors or agency personnel when something requested has not been received or when changes in pricing or routine have occurred without explanation, drawing on purchasing practices and relying on communication skills and experience *in order to* resolve problems of delivery and pricing. (PUA)

(See page 163 for additional Level 4 tasks)

Reasoning Development Level 5

Definition. Have knowledge of a field of study (engineering, literature, history, business adminstration) having immediate applicability to the affairs of the world.

Defines problems, collects data, establishes facts, and draws valid conclusions in controlled situations.

Interprets an extensive variety of technical material in books, manuals, texts, and so on.

Deals with some abstract but mostly concrete variables.

Level 5: Illustrative Tasks

Access federal and FICA general ledger accounts, compare them with payroll reports looking for adjustments to tax liability for the period, based on voided manual refund checks and/or advanced earned income credit payments, drawing on knowledge of federal regulations and accounting practices, relying on detail, and following SOP *in order to* make adjustments in general ledger that affect tax liability. (PSS)

Discuss questions and issues affecting the health and future of the agency periodically with executive staff, including funding sources, policies, procedures, new programs, and obtaining of grants, drawing on knowledge of agency and its history and relying on experience, communication, and interpersonal skills *in order to* review ongoing activities of the agency and to contribute to decisions affecting operations. (CTR)

Train/orient new and existing staff on the job, focusing on policies, procedures, and practices as they apply to the accounting department, drawing on management knowledge of the department and computer technology developments and relying on communication skills *in order to* insure that staff is trained to do the work expected and meet the goals established. (CTR)

Oversee/supervise children in walking down stairs, holding onto rails, getting to gym or outside play yard, engaging them in structured (walking balance beam, tumbling, bouncing and catching ball) and free-choice (run, ride bikes, play basketball, climbing) physical activities, drawing on knowledge of gross motor skills and their role in childhood growth *in order to* promote gross motor development and cooperative play. (HST)

Prepare/write lesson plans once a week for entire following week, developing curriculum items that will be covered in class, specifying exercises/activities to be accomplished, drawing on textbook materials and teacher training and relying on experience and instructional skills *in order to* outline classwork for students for entire week. (GED)

Develop/write an instructional manual for new computer installation, including screen images illustrating the various utilities that the client needs and can refer to as models, drawing on an understanding of client needs and computer technology and relying on writing skills and experience *in order to* facilitate the client's learning of the computer operation. (SYA)

(See pages 163–164 for additional Level 5 tasks)

Reasoning Development Level 6

Definition. Have knowledge of a field of study of the highest abstractive order (e.g., mathematics, physics, chemistry, logic, philosophy, art criticism).

Deals with nonverbal symbols in formulas, equations, or graphs.

Understands the most difficult classes of concepts.

Deals with a large number of variables and determines a specific course of action (e.g., research, production) on the basis of need.

Level 6: Illustrative Tasks

Counsel church members in spiritual and/or emotional distress, drawing on knowledge of pastoral care, counseling methods, and relevant spiritual doctrine and relying on communication skills and ability to relate to people from diverse backgrounds *in order to* attend to members' spiritual and emotional needs and to provide spiritual guidance. (MIN)

Read/evaluate various methods of conducting research of a problem, drawing on the statistical, theoretical, and methodological literature related to problem, personal knowledge and experience, and/or advice of colleagues and relying on problem-solving ability *in order to* choose a methodology that is practical, feasible, and appropriate. (ARP)

Discuss/consult with professional colleagues, students, practitioners, and/or clients about research articles, theoretical literature, and/or ideas derived from professional journals, conference proceedings, books, relying on personal experience and interpersonal and communication skills *in order to* determine areas for research among competing/different theoretical positions. (ARP)

Plan and implement a construct validation study, calculate and interpret results using a computer, drawing on theoretical relationships among variables, intuited constructs, and standard research methodologies and statistical procedures and relying on analytical and management skills *in order to* determine what characteristics the test measures. (IOP)

Select/apply statistical techniques to measure the relationship between test results and job performance criteria, drawing on knowledge of statistics and tests and measures and relying on analytical and computer skills *in order to* determine whether the test(s) predict(s) job performance. (IOP)

Conceptualize/intuit new relationships between existing and evolving analytic theories and techniques without documented precedents, relating them to organizational problems, drawing on an understanding of theory and conceptual models and relying on personal insights, experience, and analytical and writing skills *in order to* develop an approach and methodology for a demonstration project or for a research model. (TBE)

Conceive/create an original hypothesis about the nature of social-psychological problems of an ethnic or socio-economic group, drawing on an understanding of theory and conceptual models and relying on analytical and writing skills *in order to* explain factors and phenomena previously unrecognized or unaccounted for. (TBE)

Additional Illustrative Tasks: Reasoning Development

Level 2

Announce presence to client, introducing self and purpose of visit; request dogs be removed; check scope of work with client; and unload materials needed, drawing on work-order information, relying on experience and interpersonal skills, and following SOP *in order to* install locks at site. (HST)

Drill/dig out holes for lock, throw, and strike plate, on both door and jamb, using portable power drill, drilling jig, and hand tools such as chisel and hammer, following SOP *in order to* prepare for lock assembly. (HST)

Note/record training received during employment that could apply toward mandatory state alcohol and drug abuse counselor certification, drawing on counselor files *in order to* have the data available to complete the application for certification when counselor meets eligibility requirements. (SAC)

Check tires; turn on headlights, signals, wipers, and warning lights daily, drawing on knowledge of vehicle operation *in order to* make sure van is in safe working condition. (HVD)

Level 3

Cut materials such as lexan, plywood, and burglar bars to size as specified in job order, using a power chop or band saw, and load materials and tools into van, drawing on knowledge of tools and materials and relying on experience *in order to* have materials on hand for various jobs of the day. (HST)

Oversee the production of computer copies of payroll, accounts payable, and purchase orders on a weekly and biweekly basis, libraries (directories) on a daily basis, and entire system on a weekly basis, using both reels and disks, and assist in computer operation as necessary, drawing on knowledge of agency accounting system and relying on computer skills, following SOP *in order to* produce back up copies of vital data. (SYA)

Participate/interact with clients in group attending such special events as professional ball games, bowling, training classes, and picnics, modeling and monitoring positive social behaviors, drawing on knowledge and interests of clients, and relying on awareness of group interactions *in order to* promote relationship with clients and share a reward for cooperation in program(s). (STW)

Level 4

Review proposed budgets for grant proposals with project director or program analyst, prepare a spreadsheet showing anticipated costs for various categories of expenses (e.g., salaries, fringe benefits, consultants, equipment, supplies, travel, rent, utilities), referring to available reference points and guidelines including previous grants, for each category, and drawing on rules and regulations governing contracts and relying on analytical skills *in order to* compile an estimated budget for submission to granting agency. (ACT)

Test students referred by delegate agencies on their achievement in reading, math, and language skills, using standardized tests, drawing on knowledge of assessment, and relying on test administration skills and experience *in order to* determine whether their grade level has improved. (GED)

Schedule/evaluate monthly fire drills and intermittent tornado drills for Head Start sites; provide dates and times to maintenance staff and teaching staff; conduct on-site evaluations including bathroom, classroom, and office checks; and monitor time and attendance factors, drawing on knowledge of safety procedures, relying on attention to detail and observation skills, and following SOP *in order to* insure that staff and children are prepared for disaster and sites comply with state licensing regulations. (HSN)

Assist agency Head Start director in orienting parents and staff in the use of self-assessment validation instrument (SAVI), clarifying interview, observation, and documention techniques and drawing on knowledge of Head Start guidelines and SAVI procedures *in order to* insure that parents and staff are familiar with the use of the self-assessment tool. (HSN)

Arrange time and place of committee meeting on phone, prepare/write agenda, keep minutes, generate special information as requested, arrange for the copy and flow of informational materials, drawing on knowledge of committee, personal interests and requirements, sources of information and relying on written and oral communication skills *in order to* have committee meetings proceed without difficulty. (PSU)

Level 5

Conduct performance appraisals in one-on-one meetings with individual staff, discussing performance as appropriate, drawing on agency guidelines and relying on interpersonal skills *in order to* fulfill agency guidelines, provide feedback, and determine whether annual increase is merited. (CTD)

Review/backtrack the inputs that produced an apparent error on printout (e.g., accounts payable, payroll), discussing matter with appropriate subordinates such as payroll clerk and program supervisor; drawing on knowledge of agency organization, programs, and financial procedures and relying on skill in working with people *in order to* correct the error. (CAT)

Negotiate leases with building tenants and other program contractors that deliver social services, drawing on agency policies and procedures and relying on experience and negotiating skills *in order to* arrive at a financial arrangement that produces an income to run the building and insure additional services for the local population. (CTD)

Evaluate/respond to request of advocate group or coalition of groups for active participation and lobbying assistance, ask for clarification of the political or legislative issue, and attend meeting if necessary, drawing on knowledge of enabling legislation and legal limitations for political action imposed on agency and relying on political awareness and communication and interpersonal skills *in order to* determine what agency can do as an organization and what can be done by individuals. (CRS)

Present results of research to area council on priority issues such as housing and drug-related crime, including resources and funding available in the community, explaining and clarifying as necessary, drawing on knowledge of agency and community and funding sources and projects in force and relying on presentation skills *in order to* enable council to make informed decisions on priority issues. (CRS)

MATHEMATICAL DEVELOPMENT SCALE

The Mathematical Development scale is concerned with knowledge and ability to deal with mathematical problems and operations from counting and simple addition to higher mathematics.

Mathematical Development Benchmarks

Level 1

Definition.   Counts/performs simple addition and subtraction; reads, copies, and/or records figures.

Helpful Hints.   Where math is not involved or suggested in a task statement, it should nevertheless receive the Level 1 rating. The rationale is that basic counting could likely be a requirement to negotiate the environment of a job.

Level 1: Illustrative Tasks

Install door pins where existing door hinges are exposed on the outside, opening door, driving pin above each of the three hinges, closing door to get impression, reopening door and drilling 1" hole into impression, relying on experience and following SOP *in order to* secure door and prevent removal of door, even if hinge pins are removed. (HST)

Service center van: check oil, transmission fluid, and air in tires; clean inside and outside of vehicle; and keep mileage records, following SOP *in order to* insure van is in operating condition. (JAN)

Match approved requisition with numbers on computer-generated purchase order, relying on attention to detail and following agency accounting procedure *in order to* insure that they are accurate and exact. (APS)

Talk with coordinators by phone daily, logging developments (e.g., absences, sickness, personal time off, cancelation of meetings, unusual happenings), drawing on knowledge of agency personnel policies, and following SOP *in order to* insure attendance, coverage in case of absences, and documentation for personnel procedures. (HSA)

Distribute a nutrition needs questionnaire to parents upon enrollment, tally results, following SOP *in order to* determine nutrition training needs of parents. (HSN)

Mathematical Dvelopment Level 2

Definition.   Uses arithmetic to add, subtract, multiply, and divide whole numbers.

Reads scales and gauges as in powered equipment, where reading and signals are indicative of conditions and actions to be taken.

Level 2: Illustrative Tasks

Cut materials such as lexan, plywood, and burglar bars to size as specified in job order, using a power chop or band saw, load materials and tools into van, drawing on knowledge of tools and materials and relying on experience *in order to* have materials on hand for various jobs of the day. (HOT)

Watch/monitor boiler central panel, which indicates outside temperature and water temperature inside the boiler, adjusting thermal control for water temperature when necessary, drawing on knowledge of gas-operated boiler system, and following SOP *in order to* maintain heat in the building. (JAN)

Take inventory of supply room, counting and making note of shortages, informing center coordinator of needed supplies *in order to* have secretary prepare purchase requisition. (HVD)

Review physical nutrition assessment form of each child completed by parent and doctor, noting poor eating habits, blood pressure, and blood test results (e.g., high lead, low hematocrit or hemoglobin), drawing on knowledge of interpreting blood tests and level of nutrition and relying on attention to detail *in order to* assess the nutritional status of each child. (HSN)

Write/fill out monthly report forms (nutrition component and site summary), detailing component progress, financial data, number and type of meetings and training, upcoming plans, noting any special problems and relying on writing skills and SOP *in order to* keep administrators informed and up-to-date. (HSN)

Tabulate advocacy activities and services rendered at the crisis center, drawing from the intake and status reports prepared for clients and the daily log of inquiries *in order to* meet the agency's monthly report. (FAM)

Prepare/draft a radio, TV, and newspaper advertising plan that includes costs, specific media, schedules, and rationale for placement of ads, focusing on energy assistance, drawing on the guidelines of the ad assignment and relying on experience in dealing with the media *in order to* insure that the service reaches the appropriate audience. (CTD)

Obtain cost estimates from typesetting and printing vendors; arrange for type font, paper, ink, photoscreening, binding if needed, drawing on knowledge of cost limits and relying on an awareness of quality that can be expected for price and negotiating skills *in order to* prepare the purchase requisitions containing the specifications agreed on. (PIS)

Mathematical Development Level 3

Definition.   Makes arithmetic calculations involving fractions, decimals, and percentages.

Mentally acts on dimensional specifications marked on material or stakes.

Level 3: Illustrative Tasks

Test water from boiler system for temporary hardness, permanent hardness, total hardness, pH-Hydrogen Ion, sulfite M6-L, "p", alkalinity, chlorides, condensate, and total dissolved solids, using chemistry set, treating boiler with chemicals to bring solvent levels up to specifications, drawing on knowledge of chemistry involved and boiler system and relying on attention to detail *in order to* maintain water solvent levels. (JAN)

Install metal burglar bars, conduit (telescoped ¾" to 1" pipe), or angle aluminum on windows to meet different situations (e.g., burglar bars on first floor windows or windows that are nailed down), drilling holes according to template and driving screws to secure bars or using rivet in case of conduit, drawing on work-order specifications and experience and following SOP *in order to* burglar proof the residence. (HST)

Write up purchase requisitions for maintenance materials such as cleaning and bathroom supplies and replacement parts, drawing on inventory information and special requests, relying on attention to detail, and following SOP *in order to* stock necessary supplies. (JAN)

Review proposed budgets for grant proposals with project director or program analyst, prepare a spreadsheet showing anticipated costs for various categories of expenses (e.g., salaries, fringe benefits, consultants, equipment, supplies, travel, rent, utilities), referring to available reference points and guidelines including previous grants for each category, drawing on rules and regulations governing contracts and relying on analytical skills *in order to* compile an estimated budget for submission to granting agency. (APS)

Train program personnel in the use of a computer to enter and access data, using hands-on demonstration, including the use of a variety of function codes, accounting codes, and procedures, drawing on personal knowledge and experience with the computer system and relying on instructional skills *in order to* enable program personnel to maintain financial records and access master file. (ACT)

Estimate/formulate annual budgets for each of the grant areas, using a computer, making tradeoffs as necessary to stay within the guidelines for the specified programs, drawing on anticipated costs and income, projected salary increases, vendor costs, utilities, insurance, and the ceiling placed on the probable amount to be granted and relying on analytical skills *in order to* develop the optimum spending plan for the year. (CTD)

(See page 176 for additional Level 3 tasks)

Mathematical Development Level 4

Definition. Performs arithmetic and algebraic and/or geometric procedures in standard practical applications.

Level 4: Illustrative Tasks

Review existing computer files that will be an input source with department head and listen to statement of need and required output (e.g., accounting), write an appropriate program that processes the data as requested, test the program on a sample problem, review results with end user, modify as necessary, drawing on knowledge of content area and relying on programming experience and problem solving skills *in order to* prepare a program that meets specifications of end user. (SYA)

Formulate/develop simulations of computer generated data based on existing databases (e.g., anthropometric, human performance,) drawing on programming, drafting, and computer graphic techniques and relying on analytical skills *in order to* specify human factors design criteria for product being developed. (HFC)

Evaluate summary statistics in relation to trends and developments in the community, drawing on knowledge of the community and basic statistical measures and relying on analytical skills *in order to* be able to see how well community goals and objectives are being met. (IRS)

Design a computer program from scratch (e.g., food service program), where the existing data are not well organized in manual files; write a program that processes the data as requested; test the program on a sample problem; review results with end user and modify as necessary, drawing on programming experience and knowledge of content area communicated by department SMEs and relying on analytical skill and persistence *in order to* produce a program that meets the needs of the end user. (SYA)

Obtain data pertaining to angles, elevations, points, and contours, using alidade, level, transit, plane table, theodilite, electronic distance measuring equipment, and other surveying instruments, drawing on technical training, notes, sketches, and related records and relying on skill in operating measuring instruments and spatial relations ability *in order to* collect information for construction, map making, mining, and other purposes. (SUR)

Mathematical Development Level 5

Definition.   Have knowledge of advanced mathematical and statistical techniques such as differential and integral calculus, factor analysis, and probability determination.

Works with a wide variety of theoretical mathematical concepts.

Makes original applications of mathematical procedures, as in empirical and differential equations.

Level 5: Illustrative Tasks

Evaluate/analyze emergency shelter data on quarterly basis, including cross-tabulation with other factors (e.g., sex, source of income, employment, size of family), using computer and statistical software, enter and compile data monthly, drawing on knowledge of computer and statistical analysis and relying on experience and analytical skills *in order to* provide trend data to administrators and funding sources. (IRS)

Compile/evaluate the data of a needs assessment, both descriptive and statistical, using computer and advanced statistical software packages as needed, summarizing and categorizing the data, and noting specific emphasis and individual needs, drawing on knowledge of training and statistics and relying on analytical skills *in order to* design curriculum oriented to meet the specific needs of intended training groups.(TRS)

Examine/evaluate employment data obtained from protected groups, using statistical programs on computer, drawing on the standard procedures outlined in Equal Employment Opportunity Commission (EEOC) guidelines for assessing differential validity and test bias, psychometrics, statistics and relying on mathematical and analytical skills *in order to* determine whether selection instruments demonstrate adverse impact (IOP)

Design a pilot study, drawing on knowledge of industrial and organizational psychology, the organization, and psychometric considerations (e.g., reliability and validity) and relying on experience and conceptualization skills *in order to* evaluate the potential success of a specific organzational intervention. (IOP)

Analyze/evaluate completed questionnaires used in research (e.g., surveys), drawing on knowledge of the content area and statistical methodology and relying on experience and analytical skills *in order to* determine consumer preferences and attitudes toward client's product or service. (IOP)

Apply standardized mathematical formulas, principles, and methodology to technical problems in engineering and physical sciences, using a combination and sequence of computational methods including algebra, triginometry, geometry, vector analysis, and calculus, analyzing data using computer software, drawing on advanced training in mathematics and knowledge of computing equipment and relying on analytical and problem-solving skills and spatial relations ability *in order to* develop solutions to specific issues in industry and research. (MAT)

Additional Illustrative Tasks: Mathematical Development

Level 3

Present information, as requested, to accounting department personnel concerning agency purchasing policies and procedures, paying special attention to how procedural elements fit into the agency's computerized accounting system, drawing on knowledge of agency and relying on experience and presentation skills *in order to* share information concerning the joint responsibility of purchasing and accounting. (PUA)

Draw/construct charts that display the advantages, disadvantages, coverage, and cost of pension plans, including investment returns and their impact on present financial situation of the agency, using computer programs, drawing on knowledge of pension plans and relying on presentation and computer skills *in order to* assist office heads in making decisions. (PSU)

LANGUAGE DEVELOPMENT SCALE

The Language Development scale is concerned with knowledge and ability to speak, read, or write language materials from simple verbal instructions to complex sources of written information and ideas.

Language Development Benchmarks

Level 1

Definition. Cannot read or write, but can follow simple oral, pointing-out instructions.

Signs name and understands ordinary, routine agreements when explained, such as those relevant to leasing a house, employment (hours, wages, etc.), procuring a driver's license.

Reads lists, addresses, traffic signs, safety warnings.

Level 1: Illustrative Tasks

Drive van to work site in sequence determined by supervisor on basis of convenience to clients, drawing on experience as vehicle operator and knowledge of city traffic patterns *in order to* reach destination on schedule. (HST)

Install "door guard" and "jamb" (prefabricated metal devices) or repair doors and jambs that are too damaged to take a lock with new woodwork, using hand tools as required, relying on on-the-job experience, and following SOP *in order to* have a proper base for lock installation. (HST)

Unload boxes of supplies from van, carrying boxes to the supply room; open boxes and place them on shelf, distributing requested amounts of supplies to secretary at her desk or placing supplies in cabinets at copier, relying on lifting ability and following SOP *in order to* have supplies available for staff. (HVD)

Collate by hand selected documents that cannot be handled by machine, following specifications and relying on manual skills *in order to* produce an assembled product. (SWB)

Pick up newspapers at newsstand and mail at U.S. Postal Station in building, carry or drag (if very heavy) to mailroom, relying on physical strength and following SOP *in order to* have mail available for sorting and papers ready for delivery to persons designated. (SWB)

Hand deliver packages of correspondence or other material from headquarters to downtown installations on request, either by walking or using bus *in order to* expedite transmission of materials. (SWB)

Load/unload donations (mattresses, clothes) from trucks, vans, or cars, carrying to designated areas such as clients' homes, crisis centers, and homeless housing programs, drawing on knowledge of safe lifting procedures and relying on physical strength, following SOP *in order to* deliver donations to appropriate place. (JAN)

Language Development Level 2

Definition. Reads material containing short sentences, simple concrete vocabulary, words that avoid complex Latin derivatives (comic books, popular tabloids, "westerns").

Converses with service personnel (waitpersons, ushers, cashiers).

Copies ordinary, everyday written records or business letter precisely without error.

Keeps taxi driver's trip record or service maintenance record.

Level 2: Illustrative Tasks

Respond to phone call request to check possible malfunctions in heating or security systems at building at odd hours of the day or night, including weekends, drawing on familiarity with the systems and relying on attention to detail, following SOP *in order to* insure systems are functioning properly or emergency repairs are needed. (JAN)

Phone director of the Family Crisis Center daily, asking if there will be any children attending either the morning or afternoon Head Start session, relying on courtesy skills and following SOP *in order to* determine if a pick up is necessary and to insure that new children that day will be accompanied by parent. (HVD)

Announce presence to client, introducing self and purpose of visit; request dogs be removed, review scope of work with client and unload materials needed, drawing on work order information, relying on experience and interpersonal skills, and following SOP *in order to* install locks at site. (HST)

Call/visit stores, inquiring about needed parts and price, referring to type and quantity information supplied by secretary, giving information to the secretary for preparation of purchase order form, picking up supplies when paperwork has been processed, relying on oral communication skills, and following SOP *in order to* get parts needed to make repairs. (HVD)

Assign a serial number for new vendors when informed of their selection by a program area, keying number, identification, and conditions of payment into computer and following SOP *in order to* facilitate payments. (APS)

Take inventory of supply room, counting and making note of shortages and informing center coordinator of needed supplies *in order to* have secretary prepare purchase requisition. (HVD)

Type labels for individual folders for incoming material, relying on clerical skills and following SOP *in order to* prepare files for new material. (SWB)

Language Development Level 3

Definition.   Comprehends orally expressed trade terminology (jargon) of a specific technical nature.

Reads material on level of the *Reader's Digest* and straight news reporting in popular mass newspapers.

Comprehends ordinary newscasting (uninvolved sentences and vocabulary with focus on events rather than on their analysis).

Copies written material from one record to another, catching gross errors in grammar.

Fills in report forms, such as Medicare forms, employment applications, and card form for income tax.

Conducts house-to-house surveys to obtain common census-type information or market data, such as preferences for commercial products in everyday life.

Level 3: Illustrative Tasks

Write up purchase requisitions for maintenance materials such as cleaning and bathroom supplies and replacement parts, drawing on inventory information and special requests, relying on attention to detail, and following SOP *in order to* stock necessary supplies. (JAN)

Inform new parents riding in van about Head Start, telling them about various agency programs available to them (e.g., Basic Skills, Head Start), drawing on knowledge of agency and relying on courtesy and communication skills *in order to* give new parents at the Family Crisis Center general information on agency. (HVD)

Evaluate training, drawing on ratings obtained from trainees on special forms prepared for the purpose, including such factors as trainer preparation and skill, coverage of content, special materials, learning facilities, and trainee's perceived level of achievement, relying on basic statistical skills *in order to* determine the effectiveness of the training and accomplishment of objectives. (TRS)

Calculate/project on a monthly basis the kinds and amounts of food items and household issuance rates for each distribution site, drawing on knowledge of inventory on hand, projected amounts and dates of food deliveries, and projected utilization/demand at site, relying on arithmetic skills *in order to* insure all sites receive comparable food and allocations. (PSC)

Fill-in/complete forms and assign voucher number for approved bills and invoices (e.g., lease payments, consultant fees, utilities, travel advances), following agency accounting procedure and SOP *in order to* enter information into computer for issuance of checks. (APS)

Prepare/list a monthly accounts payable exception list (problem accounts), noting outstanding accounts and missing paper for forwarding to agency administrators, relying on attention to detail, and following SOP *in order to* keep administrators updated on programs that are not on track. (APS)

Sort forms monthly according to type of service rendered, drawing on the data describing the program and needs of callers, following SOP *in order to* facilitate the process of data tabulation (age of caller, zip code, type of service) for use by agency administrators and planners. (IRS)

(See page 190 for additional Level 3 tasks)

Language Development Level 4

Definition.   Writes routine business correspondence reflecting standard procedures.

Interviews job applicants to determine work best suited for their abilities and experience; contacts employers to interest them in services of agency.

Reads and comprehends technical manuals and written instructions as well as drawings associated with practicing a craft.

Conducts opinion research surveys involving stratified samples of the population.

Guides people on tours through historical or public buildings and relates relevant anecdotes and historical material.

Level 4: Illustrative Tasks

Explain/describe agency practices and reports as necessary, using phone or letter, conveying payroll files, reports, and/or documents to outside auditors as requested, drawing on knowledge of agency and relying on communication skills *in order to* facilitate their audit. (PSS)

Contact vendors by phone or in writing concerning inconsistent or incompatible commercial paper calling for payment, using form letters where available, drawing on agency accounting manual and relying on communication and writing skills *in order to* straighten out discrepancies and obtain paper that legitimizes payments. (APS)

Develop/draft monthly summary reports, using computer software (e.g., Lotus 1-2-3) showing administrative costs for the period and financial status of all agency programs, drawing on knowledge of accounting system and spreadsheet software and relying on attention to detail *in order to* submit reports to controller for approval prior to informing budget/ finance committee. (CAT)

Review educational materials and supplies described and displayed in catalogs, drawing on observed special classroom needs and relying on reading skills and experience *in order to* recommend materials for requisitioning by lead teacher. (HST)

Administer Test of Adult Basic Education (TABE) to candidates referred by various social service programs, courts, and walk-ins, drawing on knowledge of assessment, relying on experience in test administration *in order to* diagnose grade level and educational needs of individuals for placement in appropriate classes. (GED)

Prepare/write teaching sheets, daily lesson plans, and monthly reports, drawing on professional training and observed progress of class and special workshops and relying on writing skills *in order to* guide each day's work and to keep a record of teaching progress. (HST)

Participate as a member in coalitions of community groups assembled to help the poor and disadvantaged populations, drawing on knowledge of the problems of the poor and relying on communication and interpersonal skills and experience *in order to* influence the legislative process and delivery of government services. (IRS)

Review paperwork for projects being accounted for such as purchase requisitions, payment authorizations, check requests, consultant contracts and payments, travel, reimbursements; sign off and forward for disposition, following agency accounting practices *in order to* approve or reject disbursements. (ACT)

Language Development Level 5

Definition.   Writes instructions for assembly of prefabricated parts into units.

Writes instructions and specifications concerning proper use of machinery.

Writes copy for advertising.

Reports news for the newspapers, radio, or television.

Prepares and delivers lectures for audiences that seek information about the arts, sciences, and humanities in an informal way.

Level 5: Illustrative Tasks

Prepare/write an integrated report for the regional office of Head Start, reading reports, summarizing, and highlighting activities and developments, indicating plans for resolving problems, drawing on the monthly and quarterly reports and progress indicators of both agency and delegate Head Start programs, relying on writing and organization skills *in order to* keep the funding source up-to-date and informed. (HSA)

Present a verbal report on Head Start activities at monthly meeting of Child and Youth committee, and at the appropriate time of year present a briefing paper of the refunding proposal, drawing on knowledge of program and agency structure and relying on communication skills in order to keep colleagues mutually informed about developments in the child and youth area. (HSA)

Prepare/write article for newsletter and reports on home visits, parent-teacher conference, and progress of child, drawing on professional training and special workshop education, relying on writing skills, and following SOP *in order to* promote communication with parents about their children and parent involvement with Head Start activity. (HST)

Make presentations, as requested, to accounting department personnel concerning agency purchasing policies and procedures, paying special attention to how procedural elements fit into the agency computerized accounting system, drawing on knowledge and experience and relying on presentation skills *in order to* share information concerning the joint responsibility of purchasing and accounting and the effectiveness of the system. (PUA)

Confer with the leaders of government (e.g., the mayor), business, and industry (e.g., CEOs of local corporations), making presentations at formal meetings about specific needs in the community (e.g., efforts to overcome substance abuse), particularly the need for funding and/or support for community and government efforts, stressing the positive effect that a particular program can have for the community as well as recipients, drawing on knowledge and understanding of agency programs and relying on interpersonal and communication skills *in order to* obtain funds and support for agency efforts on behalf of the poor and minorities. (EXD)

Write nutrition information packets/booklets, illustrate concepts using everyday terminology, drawing on knowledge of nutrition, technical information, and needs of parents, relying on writing skills and ability to adapt materials to specific target populations *in order to* provide parents with tools for understanding nutritional concepts. (HSN)

(See pages 190–191 for additional Level 5 tasks)

Language Development Level 6

Definition.   Reports, writes, edits article for technical and scientific journal (e.g., *Journal of Educational Sociology, Science, Physical Review, Daedalus*) or journals specializing in advanced literary criticism, (e.g., *The New Yorker, New York Review of Books*).

Prepares and draws up deeds, leases, wills, mortgages, and contracts.

Prepares and delivers lectures on politics, economics, education, or science to specialized students and/or professional societies.

Comprehends and applies technical engineering data for designing buildings and bridges.

Comprehends and discusses works of a highly symbolic nature, such as works in logic and philosophy (e.g., Kant, Whitehead, Russell).

Level 6: Illustrative Tasks

Develop contracts with participating feeding sites, shelters, and pantries, specifying terms and conditions of participation in the program, conditions of storage, inventory control, and recordkeeping requirements; drawing on knowledge of program requirements and agency's contractual requirements and relying on negotiating skills *in order to* insure that the Soup Kitchen/Food Bank program operates in compliance with state and federal requirements. (PSC)

Prepare/write new proposals for new programs for agency and/or delegate agencies, drawing on statement of conceptualized objectives, needs and feasibilities, funding source requirements, and relationships with cooperating agencies, relying on writing skills *in order to* obtain money for needed services. (PSC)

Meet with financial officers, directors, contract monitors, and/or grant officers, alone or accompanied by other agency executives, regarding contract financial problems and or misunderstandings, drawing on knowledge of particular contract or agency experience and relying on negotiating skills *in order to* clarify problems and/or obtain payments. (CTR)

Meet with personnel concerned about policy and procedural issues, including financial operations, and conduct a brain-storming session on proposed revisions, drawing on knowledge of issue and relying on communication skills and sensitivity to proposals made *in order to* develop revised recommendations on policy, procedure, or methods of operation. (CTR)

Meet periodically with agency Board Committees (e.g., budget and finance, audit), presenting them with up-to-date information on the financial status and practices associated with agency, drawing on knowledge and experience with agency programs and accounting practices and relying on presentation skills *in order to* keep them informed and to obtain their recommendations or directives. (CTR)

Additional Illustrative Tasks: Language Development

Level 3

Review purchase requisition of services and goods for description and dollar amount, adherence to funding source procurement and agency approval policies, phoning vendors for current information and price as necessary; drawing on catalog resources, agency policies, and procedures and relying on attention to detail *in order to* insure accuracy and legitimacy of purchase requisition and approve it for entry into computer. (PUA)

Note/record training received during employment that could apply toward mandatory state alcohol and drug abuse counselor certification, drawing on counselor files *in order to* have the data available to complete the application for certification when counselor meets eligibility requirements. (SAC)

Level 5

Prepare/write a variety of reports, such as monthly progress reports containing budget, statistical and narrative material, quarterly reports on achievement of goals and objectives of the center, and ad-hoc reports documenting long distance calls, drawing on the center's regular documentation and required formats and funding procedures and relying on writing skills *in order to* keep agency and funding sources informed on a regular basis. (CTD)

Develop/write an instructional manual for new computer installation, including screen images illustrating the various utilities that the client needs and can refer to as models, drawing on an understanding of client needs and computer technology and relying on writing skills and experience *in order to* facilitate the client's learning of the computer operation. (SYA)

Instruct/train individuals in computer operation, in groups or one-on-one, taking them through procedures step-by-step, using prepared manual to answer questions, giving and reviewing exercises, and encouraging participants to apply training and use system as often as possible, drawing on knowledge of field and training experience and relying on communication and instructional skills *in order to* provide individuals with computer skills and knowledge. (SYA)

Conduct training sessions, using lesson plans previously designed, adapting the material to the learning rate of the participants and the questions that they raise, drawing on knowledge of content area, experience, and training as an instructor and relying on communication and presentation skills *in order to* facilitate the learning of the content by the participants. (TRS)

Delegate to staff or undertake on own the gathering of data relevant to an upcoming meeting or written appeal concerning a contract problem or misunderstanding, drawing on knowledge of particular issue/contract and agency operations and relying on personal judgment *in order to* be prepared to explain or defend agency position. (CTR)

Negotiate leases with building tenants and other program contractors that deliver social services, drawing on agency policies and procedures and relying on experience and negotiating skills *in order to* arrive at a financial arrangement that produces an income to run the building. (CTD)

APPENDIX A: COMPLETE LISTING OF FJA SCALES

THINGS FUNCTIONS SCALE

Working with Things literally means the physical interaction with tangibles, including taken-for-granted items such as desktop equipment (pencils, paper clips, telephone, handstamps, etc.), blackboards and chalk, and cars. Physical involvement with tangibles such as desktop equipment, and so on, may not seem very important in tasks primarily concerned with Data or People, but their importance is quickly apparent when handicap or ineptness occurs. An involvement with Things can be manifested in requirements for neatness, arrangements, and/or security of the workplace. Workers who make decisions or take actions concerning the disposition of Things (tools, materials, or machines) are considered to be working mainly with Data, although they physically handle Things (e.g., records, telephone, and catalogs).

> The Things Functions scale includes: physical interaction with and response to tangibles—touched, felt, observed, and related to in space; images visualized spatially.

The arabic number assigned to definitions represents the successive levels of this ordinal scale. The A, B, C, and D definitions are variations on the same level.

Level 1A: Handling

Works (cuts, shapes, assembles, etc.) digs, moves, or carries objects or materials where objects, materials, tools, and so on, are one or few in number and are the primary involvement of the worker. Precision requirements are relatively gross. Includes the use of dollies, handtrucks, and the like; writing tools, telephones, and other desktop equipment; and the casual or optional use of tools and other tangibles.

Level 1B: Feeding-Offbearing

Inserts, throws, dumps, or places materials into, or removes them from, machines, equipment, or measuring devices that are automatic or tended/operated by other workers. Precision requirements are built in, largely out of control of worker.

Level 2A: Machine Tending I—Material Products and Processing

Starts, stops, and monitors the functioning of machines and equipment set up by other workers, where the precision of output depends on keeping one to several controls in adjustment in response to automatic signals according to specifications. Includes all machine situations where there is no significant set-up or change of set-up, where cycles are very short, alternatives to nonstandard performance are few, and adjustments are highly prescribed.

Level 2B: Machine Tending II—Data Processing and Duplication

Starts, stops, monitors the functioning of machines and equipment that are preprogrammed to perform the basic functions involved in data processing, document copying, and printing. Machines/equipment are activated at keyboard terminals or touch control panels and can accomplish special effects for particular activities through the input of special codes. Nonproductive use of calculators, typewriters, and similar office equipment is included here.

Level 3A: Manipulating

Works (cuts, shapes, assembles, etc.), digs, moves, guides, or places objects or materials where objects, tools, controls, and so on, are several in number. Precision requirements range from gross to fine. Includes waiting on tables and the use of ordinary portable power tools with interchangeable parts and ordinary tools around the home such as kitchen and garden tools used for food preparation, installation, and minor repairs.

Level 3B: Operating-Controlling I

Starts, stops, controls, and adjusts a machine or equipment designed to fabricate and/or process things, data, or people. The worker may be involved in activating the machine, as in word processing or turning wood, or the involvement may occur primarily at start-up and stop, as with a semi-automatic machine. Operating a machine involves readying and adjusting the machine and/or material as work progresses. Controlling equipment involves monitoring gauges, dials, and so on, and turning valves and other devices to control such items as temperature, pressure, flow of liquids, speed of pumps, and reaction of materials. (This rating is applied only to operators of one machine or one unit of equipment).

Level 3C: Driving-Controlling

Starts, stops, and controls (steers, guides) the actions of machines in two-dimensional space for which a course must be followed to move things or people. Actions regulating controls require continuous attention and readiness of response to surface traffic conditions.

Level 3D: Starting Up

Readies powered mobile equipment for operation, typically following standard procedures. Manipulates controls to start up engines, allows for warm-up and pressure build-up as necessary, checks mobility where movement is involved and working parts (as in construction equipment), brakes, gauges indicating serviceability (fuel, pressure, temperature, battery output, etc.), and visually checks for leaks and other unusual conditions. Includes reverse shut-down procedures.

Level 4A: Precision Working

Works, moves, guides, or places objects or materials according to standard practical procedures, where the number of objects, materials, tools, and so on, embraces an entire craft and accuracy expected is within final finished tolerances established for the craft. (Use this rating where work primarily involves manual or power hand tools.)

Level 4B: Setting Up

Installs machines or equipment; inserts tools; alters jigs, fixtures, and attachments and/or repairs machines or equipment to ready and/or restore them to their proper function according to job order or blueprint specifications. Involves primary responsibility for accuracy. May involve one or a number of machines for other workers or worker's own operations.

Level 4C: Operating-Controlling II

Starts, stops, controls, and continuously modifies set-up of equipment designed to hoist and move materials or transport persons and/or materials in multidimensional space. Includes the operation of heavy equipment to reshape and/or pave the earth's surface. Manipulation of controls requires continuous attention to changing conditions and readiness of response to activate the equipment in lateral, vertical, and/or angular operations.

DATA FUNCTIONS SCALE

Data should be understood to mean information, ideas, facts, and statistics. Involvement with Data is inherent in the simplest job instruction in the form of recognizing the relationship of a tool to its function or the significance of a pointing instruction. Data are always present in a task, even though the major emphasis of the task might be dealing with Things and/or People. Where Things are primarily involved, Data tend to show up as specifications. Where People are primarily involved, Data tend to show up as information about objective events or conditions, information about feelings, or ideas that could be tinged with objective information and/or feeling. The Data Scale measures the degree to which workers might be expected to become involved with Data in the tasks they are asked to perform, from simple recognition through degrees of arranging, executing, and modifying to reconceptualizing Data.

The data functions in work and learning are the same, but there is an important difference. In work situations, the functions tend to be demarcated and allocated to specific assignments reflecting organization structure and production flow. In the learning situation, functions know no bounds. Every new learning can be a challenge involving aspects of creativity (synthesizing), hence, all subsidiary functions in the Data scale—either slowly or quickly. Thus, the Data scale basically reflects the cognitive development that occurs in human learning.

Data are information, ideas, facts, statistics, specification of output, knowledge of conditions, techniques; mental operations.

The arabic number assigned to definitions represents the successive levels of this ordinal scale. The A, B, C, and D definitions are variations on the same level.

Level 1: Comparing

Selects, sorts, or arranges data, people, or things, judging whether their readily observable functional, structural, or compositional characteristics are similar to or different from prescribed standards. Examples: checks oil level, tire pressure, worn cables; observes and responds to hand signal of worker indicating movement of load; sizes, sorts, and culls tangibles being conveyed to workers; compares lists of names and numbers for similarity.

Level 2: Copying

Transcribes, enters, and/or posts data, following a schema or plan to assemble or make things and using a variety of work aids. Transfers information mentally from plans, diagrams, instructions to workpiece or work site. Examples: attends to stakes showing a grade line to be followed while operating equipment.

Level 3A: Computing

Performs arithmetic operations and makes reports and/or carries out a prescribed action in relation to them. Interprets mathematical data on plans, specifications, diagrams, or blueprints, transferring them to workpiece; for example, reads and follows specifications on stakes.

Level 3B: Compiling

Gathers, collates, or classifies information about things, data, or people, following schema or system but using discretion in application. Examples: considers wind, weather (rain or shine), shape, weight and type of load, height, and capacity of boom in making lift using a crane; converts information in a book (title, author, subject, etc.) into a standard library code.

Level 4: Analyzing

Examines and evaluates data (about things, data, or people) with reference to the criteria, standards, and/or requirements of a particular discipline, art, technique, or craft to determine interaction effects (consequences) and to consider alternatives. Examples: considers/evaluates instructions, site and climatic conditions, nature of load, capacity of equipment, other crafts engaged with in order to situate (spot) a crane to best advantage; researches a problem in a particular subject matter area to consider and to enumerate the options available in dealing with it.

Level 5A: Innovating

Modifies, alters, and/or adapts existing designs, procedures, or methods to meet unique specifications, unusual conditions, or specific standards of effectiveness within the overall framework of operating theories, principles, and/or organizational contexts; for example, improvises, using existing attachments, or modifies customary equipment to meet unusual conditions and fulfill specifications.

Level 5B: Coordinating

Decides times, place, and sequence of operations of a process, system, or organization, and/or the need for revision of goals, policies (boundary conditions), or procedures on the basis of analysis of data and of performance review of pertinent objectives and requirements. Includes overseeing and/or executing decisions and/or reporting on events; for example, selects/proposes equipment best suited to achieve an output considering resources (equipment, costs, personnel) available to get the job done.

Level 6: Synthesizing

Takes off in new directions on the basis of personal intuitions, feelings, and ideas (with or without regard for tradition, experience, and existing parameters) to conceive new approaches to or statements of problems and the development of system, operational or aesthetic solutions or resolutions of them, typically outside of existing theoretical, stylistic, or organizational context.

PEOPLE FUNCTIONS SCALE

The substance of the live interaction between people (and animals) is communication. In the broadest sense, the communication can be verbal or nonverbal. What makes communication complex is the heavy load that messages carry, for example, Data in their objective and subjective forms—the way in which they are delivered (volume, tone, accompanying gesture, and the formal rules and informal customs that govern the context of the communication). Because there is a large subjective element on the part of both the sender and the receiver of a communication, it is very difficult to measure or to assign absolute values or primary importance to one or another type of information in the interaction.

What further complicates pinning down the nature of specific interpersonal behavior is that *affect* can serve as a tool for managing oneself in the interaction as well as the informational substance of the interaction. Affect, as information and as tool, can occur in the simplest as well as the most complex interaction. For example, affect expressed in a sulky manner, perhaps to gain attention or perhaps to express resentment on the part of a worker, can quickly become the informational substance of the interaction when the supervisor asks nonreactively, "Don't you feel well?" and gets the answer "No, I don't. My child is ill. I should be home."

The functions in the People scale deal with these complex questions only indirectly. The assumption of ordinality is more tenuous than in the Things and Data scales and depends more heavily on role, status, and authority, which are often associated with, but not necessarily a part of, skill. In effect, the functions try to capture the variety of interpersonal behavior assigned in various work situations and are more or less arranged, as in the other scales, according to the need, in general, to deal with increasing numbers of variables and with greater degrees of discretion. (The function least likely to fit this pattern is Supervising, which probably could have a scale of its own.)

Skill in dealing with people is undoubtedly as much an art as a methodology. Although measurement in this area is in a primitive state, it is essential to delineate descriptive and numerical standards by which a function can be appraised in the task in which it occurs. One should especially note cultural boundary conditions in matters of courtesy, diplomatic protocol, and "rule" of behavior in patient-doctor relationships.

The People scale measures live interaction between people, and people and animals.

Level 1A: Taking Instructions—Helping

Attends to the work assignment, instructions, or orders of supervisor. No immediate response or verbal exchange is required unless clarification of instruction is needed.

Level 1B: Serving

Attends to the needs or requests of people or animals or to the expressed or implicit wishes of people. Immediate response is involved.

Level 2: Exchanging Information

Talks to, converses with, and/or signals people to convey or obtain information or to clarify and work out details of an assignment, within the framework of well-established procedure; for example, requests clarification of a verbal signal (in person or on radio) or hand signal.

Level 3A: Sourcing Information

Serves as a primary and central source to external public or internal workforce of system information that is crucial in directing/routing people or workers to their destination or areas of concern, which makes it possible for system/organization to function. Examples: information personnel in stores and terminals; reception/routing person in large office; inventory and/or stock clerk.

Level 3B: Persuading

Influences others in favor of a product, service, or point of view by talks or demonstration. Examples: demonstrates safety procedures required on a piece of equipment for compliance with new regulations; sales personnel in hardware and furniture stores or boutiques.

Level 3C: Coaching

Befriends and encourages individuals on a personal, caring basis by approximating a peer- or family-type relationship either in a one-on-one or small group situation; gives instruction, advice, and personal assistance concerning activities of daily living, the use of various institutional services, and participation in groups. Examples: gives support or encouragement to apprentice or journeyperson on unfamiliar piece of equipment; coaches students on school athletic team or sponsors new employees in a training situation.

Level 3D: Diverting

Amuses/performs to entertain or distract individuals and/or audience or to lighten a situation. Examples: daycare teaching, storytelling, street entertaining.

Level 4A: Consulting

Serves as a source of technical knowledge and provides such knowledge as well as related ideas to define, clarify, enlarge on, or sharpen procedures, capabilities, or product specifications. Examples: informs project managers of effective and appropriate use of equipment to achieve output within constraints (time, money, etc.); presents options to solve particular problems.

Level 4B: Instructing

Teaches subject matter to others or trains others, including animals, through explanation, demonstration, and test, bringing them to a desired level of performance.

Level 4C: Treating

Acts on or interacts with individuals or small groups of people or animals who need help (as in sickness) to carry out specialized therapeutic or adjustment procedures. Systematically observes results of treatment within the framework of total personal behavior because unique individual reactions to prescriptions (chemical, physical, or behavioral) may not fall within the range of expectation/prediction. Motivates, supports, and instructs individuals to accept or cooperate with therapeutic adjustment procedures when necessary.

Level 5: Supervising

Determines and/or interprets work procedure for a group of workers, assigns specific duties to them delineating prescribed and discretionary content, maintains harmonious relations among them, evaluates performance (both prescribed and discretionary) and promotes efficiency and other organizational values; makes decisions on procedural and technical levels.

Level 6: Negotiating

Bargains and discusses on a formal basis, as a representative of one side of a transaction, for advantages in resources, rights, privileges, and/or contractual obligations, giving and taking within the limits provided by authority or within the framework of the perceived requirements and integrity of a problem.

Level 7: Mentoring

Works with individuals having problems affecting their life adjustment in order to advise, counsel, and/or guide them according to legal, scientific, clinical, spiritual, and/or other professional principles. Advises clients on implications of analyses or diagnoses made of problems, courses of action open to deal with them, and merits of one strategy over another.

Level 8: Leading

Sets forth/asserts a vision that has an impact on and defines the mission, culture, and values of an organization; sets direction, time perspective, and organizational structure for achievement of goals and objectives; models behavior that inspires and motivates achievement (distinct from management).

WORKER INSTRUCTIONS SCALE

Level 1

Inputs, outputs, tools, equipment, and procedures are all specified. Almost everything the worker needs to know is contained in the assignment. The worker usually turns out a specified amount of work or a standard number of units per hour or day.

Level 2

Inputs, outputs, tools, and equipment are all specified, but the worker has some leeway in the procedures and methods used to get the job done. Almost all the information needed is in the assignment instructions. Production is measured on a daily or weekly basis.

Level 3

Inputs and outputs are specified, but the worker has considerable freedom as to procedure and timing, including the use of tools and/or equipment. The worker may have to refer to several standard sources for information (handbooks, catalogues, wall charts). Time to complete a particular product or service is specified, but this varies up to several hours.

Level 4

Output (product or service) is specified in the assignment, which may be in the form of a memorandum or of a schematic (sketch or blueprint). The worker must work out own way of getting the job done, including selection and use of tools and/or equipment, sequence of operations (tasks), and obtaining important information (handbooks, etc.). Worker may either do the work or set up standards and procedures for others to do it.

Level 5

Same as Level 4, but in addition the workers are expected to know and employ theory so that they understand the "why's" and "wherefore's" of the various options that are available for dealing with a problem and can independently select from among them. Workers may have to do some reading in the professional and/or trade literature in order to gain this understanding and/or seek assistance from a technical "expert."

Level 6

Various possible outputs are described that can meet stated technical or administrative needs. The worker must investigate the various possible outputs and evaluate them in regard to performance characteristics and input demands. This usually requires creative use of theory well beyond referring to standard sources. There is no specification of inputs, methods, sequences, sources, or the like.

Level 7

There is some question as to what the need or problem really is or what directions should be pursued in dealing with it. In order to define the problem, to control and explore the behavior of the variables, and to formulate possible outputs and their performance characteristics, the worker must consult largely unspecified sources of information and devise investigations, surveys, or data analysis studies (strategies).

Level 8

Information and/or direction comes to the worker in terms of needs (tactical, organizational, strategic, financial). Worker must call for staff reports and recommendations concerning methods of dealing with them. He/she coordinates both organizational and technical data in order to make decisions and determinations regarding courses of action (outputs) for major sections (divisions, groups) of the organization.

REASONING DEVELOPMENT SCALE

The Reasoning Development scale is concerned with knowledge and ability to deal with theory versus practice, abstract versus concrete, and many versus few variables.

Level 1

Have the common-sense understanding to carry out simple one-or two-step instructions in the context of highly standardized situations.

Recognize unacceptable variations from the standard and take emergency action to reject inputs or stop operations.

Level 2

Have the common-sense understanding to carry out detailed but uninvolved instructions where the work involves a few concrete/specific variables in or from standard/typical situations.

Level 3

Have the common-sense understanding to carry out instruction where the work involves several concrete/specific variables in or from standard/typical situations.

Level 4

Have knowledge of a system of interrelated procedures, such as bookkeeping, internal combustion engines, electric wiring systems, nursing, farm management, ship sailing, or machining, and the ability to access optional solutions to ordinary problems.

Apply principles to solve practical everyday problems and deal with a variety of concrete variables in situations where only limited standardization exists.

Interpret a variety of instructions furnished in written, oral, diagrammatic, or schedule form.

Level 5

Have knowledge of a field of study (engineering, literature, history, business adminstration) having immediate applicability to the affairs of the world.

Define problems, collect data, establish facts, and draw valid conclusions in controlled situations.

Interpret an extensive variety of technical material in books, manuals, texts, and so on.

Deal with some abstract but mostly concrete variables.

Level 6

Have knowledge of a field of study of the highest abstractive order (e.g., mathematics, physics, chemistry, logic, philosophy, art criticism).

Deal with nonverbal symbols in formulas, equations, or graphs.

Understand the most difficult classes of concepts.

Deal with a large number of variables and determine a specific course of action (e.g., research, production) on the basis of need.

MATHEMATICAL DEVELOPMENT SCALE

The Mathematical Development scale is concerned with knowledge and ability to deal with mathematical problems and operations from counting and simple addition to higher mathematics.

Level 1

Counting to simple addition and subtraction, reading, copying, and/or recording of figures.

Level 2

Use arithmetic to add, subtract, multiply, and divide whole numbers.

Reading scales and gauges as in powered equipment where reading and signals are indicative of conditions and actions to be taken.

Level 3

Make arithmetic calculations involving fractions, decimals, and percentages. Mentally act on dimensional specifications marked on material or stakes.

Level 4

Perform arithmetic and algebraic and/or geometric procedures in standard practical applications.

Level 5

Have knowledge of advanced mathematical and statistical techniques such as differential and integral calculus, factor analysis, and probability determination.

Work with a wide variety of theoretical mathematical concepts.

Make original applications of mathematical procedures, as in empirical and differential equations.

LANGUAGE DEVELOPMENT SCALE

The Language Development scale is concerned with knowledge and ability to speak, read, or write language materials from simple verbal instructions to complex sources of written information and ideas.

Level 1

Cannot read or write but can follow simple oral, pointing-out instructions.

Sign name and understand ordinary, routine agreements when explained, such as those relevant to leasing a house, employment (hours, wages, etc.), or procuring a driver's license.

Read lists, addresses, traffic signs, safety warnings.

Level 2

Read material containing short sentences, simple concrete vocabulary, words that avoid complex Latin derivatives (comic books, popular tabloids, "westerns").

Converse with service personnel (waitpersons, ushers, cashiers).

Copy ordinary, everyday written records or business letter precisely without error. Keep taxi driver's trip record or service maintenance record.

Level 3

Comprehend orally expressed trade terminology (jargon) of a specific technical nature.

Read material on level of the *Reader's Digest* and straight news reporting in popular mass newspapers.

Comprehend ordinary newscasting (uninvolved sentences and vocabulary with focus on events rather than on their analysis).

Copy written material from one record to another, catching gross errors in grammar.

Fill in report forms, such as Medicare forms, employment applications, and card form for income tax.

Conduct house-to-house surveys to obtain common census-type information or market data, such as preferences for commercial products in everyday life.

Level 4

Write routine business correspondence reflecting standard procedures.

Interview job applicants to determine work best suited for their abilities and experience; contact employers to interest them in services of agency.

Read and comprehend technical manuals and written instructions as well as drawings associated with practicing a craft.

Conduct opinion research surveys involving stratified samples of the population.

Guide people on tours through historical or public buildings and relate relevant anecdotes and historical material.

Level 5

Write instructions for assembly of prefabricated parts into units.

Write instructions and specifications concerning proper use of machinery.

Write copy for advertising.

Report news for the newspapers, radio, or television.

Prepare and deliver lectures for audiences that seek information about the arts, sciences, and humanities in an informal way.

Level 6

Report, write, edit article for technical and scientific journal (e.g., *Journal of Educational Sociology, Science, Physical Review, Daedalus*) or journals specializing in advanced literary criticism (e.g., *The New Yorker, New York Review of Books*).

Prepare and draw up deeds, leases, wills, mortgages, and contracts.

Prepare and deliver lectures on politics, economics, education, or science to specialized students and/or professional societies.

Comprehend and apply technical engineering data for designing buildings and bridges.

Comprehend and discuss works of a highly symbolic nature, such as works in logic and philosophy (e.g., Kant, Whitehead, Russell).

Appendix B: Comparison of Worker Function Scales

FJA and DOT,[1] CCDO,[2] and NOC[3]

FJA		DOT, CCDO, NOC	
Code	*Function*	*Code*	*Function*
Things			
4	a Precision Working	0	Setting Up
	b Setting Up	1	Precision Working
	c *Operating Controlling II*	2	Operating-Controlling
3	a Manipulating	3	Driving-Operating
	b Operating Controlling I		(Driving-Controlling—U.S.A.)
	c Driving-Controlling	4	Manipulating-Operating
	d *Starting Up*		(Manipulating—U.S.A.)
2	a Machine Tending I	5	Tending
	b *Machine Tending II*	6	Feeding-Offbearing
1	a Handling	7	Handling
	b Feeding-Offbearing	8	No Significant Relationship
Data			
6	Synthesizing	0	Synthesizing
5	a *Innovating*	1	Coordinating
	b Coordinating	2	Analyzing
4	Analyzing	3	Compiling
3	a Computing	4	Computing
	b Compiling	5	Copying
2	Copying	6	Comparing
1	Comparing	7	—
		8	No Significant Relationship

(Continued)

FJA and DOT,[1] CCDO,[2] and NOC[3]
(Continued)

	FJA			*DOT, CCDO, NOC*
Code	*Function*		*Code*	*Function*
People				
8	*Leading*		0	Mentoring
7	Mentoring		1	Negotiating
6	Negotiating		2	Instructing—Consulting
5	Supervising			(Instructing —U.S.A.)
4	a Consulting		3	Supervising
	b Instructing		4	Diverting
	c *Treating*		5	Persuading
3	a *Sourcing Information*		6	Speaking-Signalling
	b Persuading		7	Serving
	c *Coaching*		8	No Significant Relationship
	d Diverting			
2	Exchanging Information			
1	a Taking Instructions—Helping			
	b Serving			

[1]*Dictionary of Occupational Titles*—U.S.A.
[2]*Canadian Classification and Dictionary of Occupations.*
[3]*National Occupational Classification (Canada).*

Explanatory Notes for Table

1. The reason the scales are *similar* is that they originated with the same person, namely myself, the senior author of this document. I conceived and directed the research on the Functional Occupational Classification Project from 1950–1959 and received the Merit Award from the Department of Labor for this work in 1959 shortly before taking leave to matriculate for my doctorate.

2. The reasons for the *differences* are as follows: (a) FJA has grown over the years and (b) the government classifications have remained where I left them 35 years ago.

Eight additional functions (italicized in the table) have been added to the FJA Scales. *Operating-Controlling II* and *Starting Up* emerged from 10 years of consulting and development work with the International Union of Operating Engineers. *Machine Tending II* emerged as the result of technological developments in offices 1965–1985 and extensive consulting with telephone companies among others. *Sourcing Information* had similar origins.

Innovating emerged from consulting and developmental work at research laboratories and engineering companies during the early 1960s when the search became intense for creative people. *Treating* and *Coaching* emerged from work with social service agencies with treatment facilities. Leading emerged from intensive study of the leaders/executives of a social service agency (1990) and extensive studies on leadership in the literature.

In every instance the additional functions had to be defined to fill a distinct niche in the ordinal scales for Things, Data, and People. They also had to prove themselves useful in classifying what workers did. In a few instances adjustments had to be made to existing definitions.

3. Another difference is the placement of the scales with relation to each other. In FJA the placement is Things, Data, People *not* Data, People, Things as in the government classifications.

The reason for the FJA placement is the observation made very early that functioning with regard to Data is central to human functioning. Thus, it was observed that as functional complexity increased for Things and People, functional complexity increased for Data as well. However, increases in functional complexity for Data were not necessarily accompanied by parallel increases in Things and People. This observation strengthened understanding as to why people were classified as homo sapiens.

The explanation given to me in the early 1960s as to why the Data, People, Things arrangement was preferred and why the functions were coded in inverse order to their complexity was that it was necessary to keep the occupational codes in the revised DOT as close to the codes in the old DOT as possible. By assigning low numbers for high-level functions, the first digit of the second part of the code could correspond closely to the original coding system of the DOT (which was not really much of a system in the first place). This, it was felt, would make it unnecessary to effect tremendous anticipated changes in the coding structure. At the time I was about to publish the FJA version of the scales through the W.E. Upjohn Institute for Employment Research where I was employed. I was requested to keep the same order as the DOT to avoid confusion. I agreed. This was a regrettable mistake because the FJA arrangement and coding had a sound theoretical and empirical basis unlike the government rationale. Actually, changes had to be made in the coding of jobs in the DOT anyway.

4. It will be noted that the government coding is in a linear sequence as though all the functions fell into a true ordinal scale. Work with the scales during the decade of the 1960s did not support this total ordinality. Thus, in FJA, the functions are grouped according to what was empirically determined to be their ordinality. For example, the reason there are four functions on the third level and three on the fourth level of the Things Scale is that those grouped functions were more or less homogeneous as far as degree of complexity was concerned (training time, aptitude, experience). The same is true for the grouped functions in the other scales.

5. "No significant relationship." This concept does not occur in FJA for a very good reason. FJA is a holistic concept. It is assumed that a person is totally involved, 100%—physically, mentally, and interpersonally—in all tasks although in varying degrees. A lesser involvement is indicated by a lower percentage, the lowest being 5%. FJA regards it as significant if some part of the person, let us say mental, is involved in a very low amount. This is an imbalance that has consequences. In fact, the origins of the gathering movement of employee involvement and worker participation in management, using the whole person on the job, may in part be due to this concept in FJA which was asserted 45 years ago. A perusal of some of the jobs in the DOT that are coded as having "no significant relationship" will reveal the questionable tenability of this classification.

Appendix C: Task Bank for Functional Job Analyst (KSAs, Task Statements, and FJA Ratings Only)

KNOWLEDGES

- FJA model/method: training and certification
- FJA scales
- Group dynamics
- Job analysis: purpose and applications in human resource management, for example, selection, training, job design
- Role of job analyst/consultant
- Human rights legislation
- Professional/ethical guidelines
- Validation methodolgy for selection instruments

SKILLS/ABILITIES

- Listening skills
- Facilitation skills (engaging SMEs in a creative endeavor); develop rapport, handle group dynamics with sensitivity to individual feelings
- Writing skills: grammar and verbal proficiency
- Organization skills: time management
- Presentation skills
- Memory
- Word processing skill
- Cognitive agility: thinking quickly on one's feet
- Attention to detail
- Initiative, flexibility, adaptability

FUNCTIONAL JOB ANALYST TASK BANK

1.0. Planning

1.1. Contact/write workshop participants (SMEs) with invitational letter, drawing on list of employees provided by management, knowledge of job analyst's role, and the need for a representative sample of SMEs, relying on written communication skills *IOT** provide SMEs with preliminary information about FJA, encourage their attendance, and inform them of their expected active role in the workshop.

T	D	P	T	D	P	WI	R	M	L
2	3B	2	20	50	30	3	3	3	4

1.2. Schedule time, location, and facility arrangements or review client arrangements of same, using discretion, drawing on knowledge of group dynamics, organization's needs and preferences (e.g., on- or off-site location, work scheduling demands), awareness of special needs of workshop participants (e.g., handicaps), and physical layout of workshop facility, relying on time management and interpersonal skills *IOT* insure suitable time, location, and arrangements for the FJA workshop.

T	D	P	T	D	P	WI	R	M	L
1	5b	2	10	60	30	4	4	1	4

1.3. Gather/review informational materials such as the organization's job descriptions, technical training manuals, policies/procedures, drawing on training in job analyst's role and FJA model and relying on attention to detail *IOT* prepare for FJA workshop with SMEs.

T	D	P	T	D	P	WI	R	M	L
1	3b	2	10	80	10	4	3	1	4

1.4. Prepare/construct several flip charts prior to workshop session, including name of workshop and job analyst, the five (5) questions that serve as agenda for workshop and the FJA model of a task statement, drawing on FJA model and training and relying on writing (legibility) and presentation skills *IOT* to have materials ready for introductory presentation to SMEs.

T	D	P	T	D	P	WI	R	M	L
1	2	1a	40	40	20	3	2	1	3

*An alternative way of expressing *in order to*.

2.0. Facilitation

2.1. Introduce self to SMEs, asking SMEs to introduce themselves and whether they have questions about invitational letter, informing them of breaks and workshop duration, drawing on training in FJA model and relying on ability to establish rapport, presentation, and interpersonal skills *IOT* provide basic information about the FJA workshop and establish an atmosphere conducive to working together.

T	D	P	T	D	P	WI	R	M	L
1	3b	4a	5	30	65	4	4	1	4

2.2. Present charts to SMEs prepared in 1.4, noting that five (5) questions will serve as the agenda for the workshop, and that the task statement model will serve as the basis for organizing the information they provide in response to the question "What Do You Do?", drawing on training in FJA model and experience and relying on presentation skills *IOT* provide information to SMEs about the objectives, expectations, and structure of the workshop.

T	D	P	T	D	P	WI	R	M	L
1	3b	4a	5	30	65	4	4	1	4

2.3. Ask first question, "What Do You Get Paid For?", listen to responses and write responses as given on flip chart, using SMEs words; avoid being critical or judgmental; ask for clarification where there seems to be overlap, and continue until the SMEs indicate they have run out of ideas, drawing on FJA model, experience, and previous review of background material and relying on language, writing, and facilitation skills *IOT* obtain a list of Outputs to serve as an agenda for workshop and a basis for tracking 95% of work performed by SMEs.

T	D	P	T	D	P	WI	R	M	L
1	4	4a	15	35	50	5	4	1	4

2.4. Ask next two questions, repeating them as listed on prepared chart, writing Knowledges and Skills/Abilities on two separate charts, again listening to and listing responses without criticism, asking for specificity and clarification when generalities, acronyms, and abbreviations are offered, and continuing until there is a lull, drawing on FJA model and relying on language, writing, and facilitation skills IOT obtain a list of the Knowledges, Skills/Abilities essential to produce the Outputs listed in 2.3.

T	D	P	T	D	P	WI	R	M	L
1	3b	4a	15	35	50	4	4	1	4

2.5. Review/remind the SMEs of the structure and content of a task statement, referring to the chart used at the start, and that the list of Outputs will serve as the agenda, present a sample task statement if available (optional), and note that the knowledges drawn on to effect an action will be preceded by d.o. (drawing on) and the skills by r.o. (relying on), drawing on FJA model and relying on facilitation skills *IOT* alert the SMEs how the information they provide will be written up on the charts.

T	D	P	T	D	P	WI	R	M	L
1	3b	4a	5	30	65	4	3	1	4

2.6. Ask SMEs which Output they would like to start with (reinforcing their ownership of the data developed), listen for a consensus, feed back what consensus appears to be, and proceed to note it on the chart, drawing on the FJA model and awareness of group dynamics and relying on facilitation skills *IOT* get the group started in producing task data.

T	D	P	T	D	P	WI	R	M	L
1	3b	4a	5	30	65	4	4	1	4

2.7. Ask SMEs to give a brief outline of the Output, making notes to self on a flip chart, taking time and not pushing for closure so that SMEs can work out together the order and/or sequence of behaviors and intermediate results that are involved in producing the Output, drawing on the FJA model and relying on facilitation skills *IOT* get a preliminary idea of the number of tasks involved in the output and the work that needs to be done to get the tasks down in detail. (This procedure tends to reinforce the validity of the Output.)

T	D	P	T	D	P	WI	R	M	L
1	3b	4a	5	30	65	4	4	1	4

2.8. Listen actively, ask questions to distinguish worker behaviors from results, probe for indicators (procedures, guidelines, self-instruction) of instructional level, recording information expressed by SMEs in appropriate sections of the task statement and reading back task information to SMEs for approval, drawing on the FJA training, experience, and relying on analytical and facilitation skills *IOT* to produce complete task statements acceptable to the SMEs.

T	D	P	T	D	P	WI	R	M	L
1	4	4a	5	40	55	5	5	1	4

2.9.   Review/check task information as it is gathered, requesting additional information from SMEs as necessary, drawing on FJA model and relying on analytical skill *IOT* produce a task statement in which behavior is translatable to a worker function and has a result related to the orientation of the task (e.g., a primarily thing behavior has a thing result).

T	D	P	T	D	P	WI	R	M	L
1	4	4a	5	40	55	5	5	1	4

2.10.   Request examples of specific content illustrating connection between behaviors and results and recording differences among SMEs to show range functional performances can have, drawing on the FJA model, training, and experience and relying on facilitation skills *IOT* produce a database for rating tasks on all the FJA scales and to have SMEs note the broad applicability of the Task Bank.

T	D	P	T	D	P	WI	R	M	L
1	3b	4a	5	30	65	4	4	1	4

2.11.   Describe/introduce the Performance Standards segment of FJA workshop when the SMEs indicate that they have no more task data to provide for the Outputs, calling attention to the standards they may have already mentioned, stating that what is wanted here are both the standards they expect of themselves and those of management, drawing on the FJA model, training, and experience and relying on facilitation skills *IOT* obtain data indicating the standards SMEs work to.

T	D	P	T	D	P	WI	R	M	L
1	3b	4a	5	30	65	4	4	1	4

2.12.   Note/record obstacles encountered and adaptations made by the SMEs in their work, using a separate flip chart, presenting them at the conclusion of the collection of performance standards, and asking whether there are any additional obstacles they would care to add, that they need to overcome to achieve the standards nevertheless, drawing on the FJA model, training, and experience and relying on facilitation skills *IOT* obtain data for an adjunct report concerning adaptations and adjustments SMEs make to get work done.

T	D	P	T	D	P	WI	R	M	L
1	4	4a	5	30	65	5	5	1	4

2.13. Monitor/respond to group processes, for example, conversation and laughter among SMEs, differences of opinion on how things are done, questions about the FJA process, active participation by some individuals and relatively little by others, drawing on active listening, training, and experience and relying on group process skills such as eye contact, smiling, directly addressing individuals, acceptance and acknowledgment of contributions, asking for clarifications or expansion of contributions, avoiding put-downs for any reason *IOT* sustain rapport, ensure the workshop stays on track, and provide motivational feedback to SMEs.

T	D	P	T	D	P	WI	R	M	L
1	4	4a	5	15	80	5	5	1	4

2.14. Debrief SMEs (e.g., inform them of upcoming stages in the FJA process, repeat as requested the purpose of the job analysis) drawing on knowledge of the FJA model, conversations with management and relying on sensitivity to individual concerns and group process skills *IOT* insure SMEs are satisfied with their participation in the workshop and that the job analysis could not have been produced without their input.

T	D	P	T	D	P	WI	R	M	L
1	4	4a	5	15	80	4	4	1	4

3.0. Editing

3.1. Transcribe FJA using word processing equipment as available, drawing on knowledge of FJA format and relying on word processing skills *IOT* produce FJA document (Task Bank) including Outputs, Knowledges, Skills/Abilities, Task Statements, and Performance Standards for editing.

T	D	P	T	D	P	WI	R	M	L
2b	2	1a	55	35	10	3	2	1	2

3.2. Edit/revise document as necessary, avoiding any major changes to language produced in conjunction with SMEs, transcribe changes using word processing, drawing on knowledge of English language and grammar, FJA style, and method and relying on writing, word processing, time management, and occupational classification skills *IOT* produce preliminary FJA Task Bank for SME validation.

T	D	P	T	D	P	WI	R	M	L
2b	4	1a	20	65	15	5	4	2	5

4.0. Validating Task Bank

4.1. Prepare FJA document for validation; add Table of Contents, Notes Section, Instructions for editing and modifications, organize KSA sections to serve as Training Needs Survey, using word processing equipment, drawing on knowledge of Task Bank format and procedure, relevant professional guidelines, and procedures (e.g., Code of Ethics, human rights legislation, confidentiality) and relying on word processing and sensitivity to group *IOT* produce a preliminary copy of the FJA document for SME validation, sign-off, and acquisition of additional information useful to management.

T	D	P	T	D	P	WI	R	M	L
2b	3b	3a	20	65	15	4	3	1	4

4.2. Send/deliver FJA validation document to SMEs using available delivery methods, requesting direct return to FJA Analyst, drawing on knowledge of organization's policies and procedures and job analyst's role and relying on communication and interpersonal skills *IOT* fulfill the commitment to SMEs for their validation and final editing of the document and help insure the document's legal defensibility.

T	D	P	T	D	P	WI	R	M	L
1	2	1b	60	20	20	2	2	1	2

4.3. Edit/rewrite FJA task bank, integrating SMEs feedback (written comments on their edited copies), checking back with SMEs as necessary by phone or in writing, drawing on knowledge of human rights legislation, job analyst's role, and validation methods and relying on word processing and writing skills *IOT* produce a final, validated, and legally defensible document.

T	D	P	T	D	P	WI	R	M	L
2b	4	2	20	65	15	5	4	1	5

5.0. Reporting

5.1. Write report including purpose of job analysis, FJA methodology, legal defensibility, validation findings, as appropriate, using word processing equipment, drawing on knowledge of job analyst's job, purpose of job analysis with the organization, human rights legislation, relevant professional guidelines, and human resource management principles and relying on writing and analytical skills *IOT* to fulfill contractual requirements and needs of the organization and provide a basis for applications of the job analysis data (e.g., performance appraisal, personnel selection, employment equity, training, and job design).

T	D	P	T	D	P	WI	R	M	L
2b	5b	4a	20	65	15	5	5	2	5

Summary Profile (see Appendix E, pp. 234–235)

T	D	P	T	D	P	WI	R	M	L
2b	5b	4a	10	30	60	5	5	3	5

Appendix D: The Origin and Nature of Functional Job Analysis*

The idea of "origins" intrigued me and has been the trigger for this paper. I wondered whether I really knew the origins of Functional Job Analysis (FJA). In any case I decided to give it a try and attempt to provide background for some of the core concepts of FJA that seem to have made an impression on industrial and counseling psychology. The core concepts tell a great deal about its nature.

First, what are the core concepts? In the time allotted I shall dwell on seven, which is, as you know, a rather magic number. They are listed as follows:

SEVEN CORE CONCEPTS OF FJA

1. What workers do (behaviors) versus what gets done (results).
2. Things, Data, People (the objects of work).
3. Worker instructions (prescription vs. discretion).
4. Adaptive skills as driver for functional and specific content skills.
5. FJA as a systems approach (linking behavior, KSAs, results).
6. The FJA focus group interview.
7. FJA, a holistic concept.

Origins, after all, have both proximal and distal aspects. Surely who I am and where I came from have something to do with my more than 40-year exploration of FJA. It has been a labor of love, an edifice that I have

---

*This is a reprint of a paper by Sidney A. Fine presented at the centennial convention of the American Psychological Association, Washington, DC, August 15, 1992, at the Washington Hilton Hotel.

enjoyed building, an activity that has absorbed both my intellectual and aesthetic abilities.

I am a child of the 20th century, a first generation American of an idealistic Jewish family that began its life in America in New York's East Side ghetto and worked its way up to slightly less ghettoized circumstances in the East Bronx. The idealism included a strong belief in education and socialism as a means for achieving a better life for working people. My parents encouraged me to obtain a good education, stressing that this was one of the wonderful things about America, and nurtured me through public school.

I was fortunate to be admitted to Stuyvesant High School, where I obtained a grounding in engineering, science, architecture, and ultimately admission to the City College of New York. There I received a wonderful education primarily in logic, scientific method, and philosophy. I attended City College during the height of the depression and was advised to drop engineering because the field offered few opportunities to Jews, and there were no job openings anyway.

I chose philosophy, in my father's view a useless, impractical pursuit, because I could study with Morris Raphael Cohen, one of the outstanding philosophers of his day. Actually, my work with Professor Cohen was probably the most practical training I ever received for the work I was to do, but I did not know it at the time. I also developed an active interest in labor unions and liberal causes that seemed to be contributing to a better world. Despite Professor Cohen's questioning the idea of progress as a reality, I believed in it passionately.

At City College I also obtained a master's degree in clinical psychology and did a 1-year internship at a psychiatric clinic in a prison environment. At the conclusion of that stint I decided I was quite unsuited for probing other people's psyches.

When the opportunity presented itself to obtain a professional position in occupational research at the Department of Labor, I jumped at it. That was in 1940 and the beginning of my career as an industrial psychologist. That is when Ernie[1] and I met and started doing research together. We researched the reliability of estimates of job characteristic requirements used to develop job families.

As I said, I was a child of my times. Born during World War I, I was destined to be a soldier in World War II. During my service I applied my job–family experience to develop a classification system for military occupational specialties. I also earned my battle stars in the South Pacific Theatre of Operations and came home to resume my career. Shortly after, in 1948, drawing on the whole range of my life experience, including my

---

[1]Reference is to Ernest Primoff, my co-presenter.

job–family work in the armed forces, I prepared a proposal within the Department of Labor to undertake research into a Functional Occupational Classification Project (FOCP)—the purpose being to develop a classification system for the Dictionary of Occupational Titles on a scientific basis. It was accepted and modestly financed. I was first assistant director and then director of the project from 1950 to 1959.

My grounding in science and engineering predisposed me to theory and measurement and probably had something to do with my distaste for the speculative world of clinical psychology. My study of architecture, logic, and scientific method had a lot to do with my interest and pursuit of a scientific basis for occupational classification. My interest in labor unions and the working class from which I sprang oriented me to the study of work. As you can see I was grounded for the work I ultimately did in occupational classification and FJA. Nothing seems to have been wasted. It was meant to be. Lucky me.

We now turn to the seven core concepts of FJA.

What Workers Do Versus What Gets Done

Job families were constructed on the basis of common characteristics between jobs. There were the obvious content similarities involving machines, tools, work aids and materials, services, products, and subject matter. But this was not enough. We wanted them to be related on the basis of common worker characteristics because this would provide a much broader basis for suggesting transfers. Although some jobs might vary in content, they nevertheless might require similar worker characteristics and thereby make for effective transfers. This idea was strongly promoted by William Stead, one of the original directors of the occupational research project in the U.S. Employment Service. He used as an example of what he meant the likelihood of an effective transfer of textile winders who were being laid off to armature winders in an electrical plant where opportunities were cropping up. The relationship here would be on the basis of finger dexterity, eye–hand coordination, and experience with repetitive, short-cycle work.

To assist in this job–family endeavor, we had a limited number of Worker Characteristic Checklists that had been completed by job analysts in the field. These checklists were an adaptation of Viteles Psychograph and provided measures on 47 traits. Both the job content and the worker characteristic information was punched on the edges of speed sort cards, thus providing a means to sort for common characteristics among jobs.

During the job–family work we had used the gerund verb form—verbs ending in *ing* such as *feeding, tending, operating,* or *setting-up*—to indicate different levels of worker relationships to machines. These verbs tended to represent stable patterns of worker characteristics. I referred to such gerunds as "what workers do" verbs in contrast to similar verb forms such as machining, typing, and selling, which were used as descriptors of work performed on the job. These latter gerunds I called "what got done verbs." Although the former were available in the job descriptive material for machine operating jobs in the DOT, they were not available for any other jobs in an equally systematic manner.

Their value and simplicity was so great for establishing relationships that I set about looking for similar verbs among clerical jobs. I did a massive study in this area and found what I was looking for. (This was the study that led to the FOCP proposal.) At the same time I also found verbs that applied to jobs primarily involved with people. What was amazing to me was that although we had hundreds of verbs to describe the nature of work done, there were only a handful available to describe what workers do. But this handful performed the same function as those describing a relationship to machines—namely, they clued you in to the pattern of worker characteristics likely to obtain for those jobs. The current version has 32 verbs. The original version had 26. This is remarkable stability over a period of more than 40 years.

A major breakthrough had been achieved. The language of job analysis would never be the same again. All subsequent writing and research would refer to "worker-oriented variables" and "work-content variables" with or without appropriate credit to this work at the U.S. Employment Service.

Things—Data—People (The Objects of Work)

There are two more things we need to note on this transparency that originated at the same time: The verbs are organized in ordinal hierarchies and related to Things–Data–People. These two characteristics of what workers do emerged naturally along with the discovery of the verbs themselves.

That they should be arranged in ordinal hierarchies was evident from the patterns of characteristics that the verbs related to. The higher on the scale, the more training and education was indicated as well as higher cognitive requirements. In addition, the higher on the scale, the more work design shifted from repetitive-short cycle to variety and change, from primarily following specific instructions to increased use of judgment.

Could we define these verbs so they would clearly and realistically reflect these findings? This was not as easy as it seemed. We started with the regular dictionary definitions of these verbs and then shaped them to fit our conviction that we were on the right track. Each definition was formulated to include the lower function conceptually but exclude the higher function. In some cases we had to invent verbs to express the functions we had in mind such as *precision working* and *exchanging information*. In other cases we selected relatively obscure verbs such as *mentoring* and defined them to suit our function. (It is interesting that over the years mentoring has become a much more widely used verb especially in discussions of educational reform.)

How come the verbs related only to Things, Data, and People? Apparently because the job definitions that we were working with had as their objects Things, Data, and People. Please note that at the same time we were listing the Materials, Products, Services, and Subject Matters with which the jobs were involved. These, in one form or another, were the objects of the actions involved in the functions. I latched onto this discovery with enthusiasm because it appeared to embrace a universe and had overtones of that wonderful game of our childhood, namely, animal, vegetable, or mineral. More than that, I felt I was in the shoes of that famous chemist, Mendeleyev, who had discovered the Periodic Table of Elements, whereby you could predict the characteristics of still undiscovered elements. (Indeed, in the early 1960s, I gave a paper at the APA describing the use of the Structure of Worker Functions to predict where automation would strike, and I may add that I predicted correctly.)

The power of this discovery and the structure was enormous. Ultimately it meant that by selecting the appropriate function from each of the three hierarchies to describe what was getting done in a job, you were describing the relation of that job to all possible human functions in all jobs. By saying that a job involved the worker in operating controlling, computing, and exchanging information, you said that it involved all the lower functions and excluded all the higher functions. Thus, functional analysis opened up the possibility of measurement—of determining the validity and reliability of job analysis observations. In addition, because our estimates of worker characteristics dealt with physical, mental, and interpersonal potentialities, it was evident that these requirements corresponded to their Things, Data, and People objects.

Recently I had the experience of reading an interview with Isaiah Berlin, one of the outstanding philosophers of our time. Perhaps you can imagine how I felt when I read the following:

> I think that self-understanding is one of the main purposes of philosophy. One of the aims of philosophy is to understand the relationships of people, things, and words to one another.... I cannot sum up all of my beliefs in two words, but I think that all there is in the world is persons and things and ideas in people's heads—goals, emotions, hopes, fears, choices, imaginative visions, and all other forms of human experience. That is all I am acquainted with. ("Interview," 1992)

(Berlin expressed this view speaking as an empiricist and as one who rejected the idea of a world of absolute values, of good and evil, right and wrong.)

Worker Instructions (Prescription vs. Discretion)

The Scale of Worker Instructions emerged as a response to an inadequacy of the functional analysis I was doing of electronic technicians, engineers, and physicists at a major research laboratory 33 years ago. After determining the functions involved in these jobs, it was clear I was missing something that was part of the jobs in that environment—something crucial to understanding them. This was the differential allocation of responsibility. When I pursued this with management and the incumbents it turned out that the different levels of responsibility inhered in the instructions they were given and the expectations that followed. I devised the Scale of Worker Instructions to reflect these varying instructions.

Shortly after, I came across the work of Eliot Jaques and Wilfred Brown in England and their concept of Prescription/Discretion as it figured into instructions given to workers. I saw in their work a more sophisticated version of what I was trying to express and immediately merged the two, recasting my scale to reflect this new information.

This scale has turned out to be a sort of bellwether for the other scales. It has also provided enormous insight into the ways in which supervision and management operates to maintain control, often adversely affecting their own interests. For example, they will assign high level data and people functions such as analyzing and innovating, consulting, treating, and teaching—all of which require relatively high levels of discretion—but nevertheless seek to control functioning through high degrees of prescription as well as non-acknowledgment or appreciation of the discretion (judgment) exercised. This results in supervisors and workers being at cross purposes with one another.

It is worthy of note that the movement toward worker participation in management, allowing more discretion to workers on the line, and about which you have heard so much in the past 20 years, is basically a movement to correct this anomaly. In a small way, the understanding provided by the Scale of Worker Instructions in the organizations where I have worked has contributed to this movement.

Adaptive Skills as Driver for Functional and Specific Content Skills

The idea of Adaptive Skills came to me in a flash of understanding while riding on a bus to work early one morning in the summer of 1970. At the time I was employed as a research scientist at the W.E. Upjohn Institute for Employment Research. I had written a brochure entitled "Guidelines for the Employment of the Culturally Disadvantaged," an awful title using jargon left over from the War on Poverty. Essentially this document was an extension of an earlier brochure entitled "Guidelines for the Design of New Careers." It described, among other things, how the functional concepts of FJA could be used to break down complex jobs into simpler components, for example, in the service professions, to design entry jobs for persons with relatively little work experience.

It also suggested that the redesign process would provide new insights into the work itself, possibly even from the entry-level applicants who would be employed in the new jobs. On the strength of these writings, which I may add, priced at 25 cents each, were best sellers at the Upjohn Institute, Dr. Herbert Striner, my boss, suggested I meet with the Reverend Leon Sullivan, the originator of the Opportunities Industrialization Centers, whom he knew well. "He is having some problems placing his trainees. Perhaps you can be of help," he said. I went to Philadelphia, met with Rev. Sullivan, a giant of a man not only in stature but in presence and ideas, and visited a couple of the centers with him. They were excellent training institutes.

During the visits he told me that despite the excellent training provided in mechanics, office work, food services, and the like, the trainees had difficulty in adjusting to actual jobs.

Specific problems included getting to work on time, regular attendance, dress, responding to authority, and getting along with white co-workers. Simply lecturing about these matters to the trainees did not solve the problem. Rev. Sullivan was clearly frustrated. Could I help? At that point I could not. I too felt frustrated because the conventional understanding that the problem with the disadvantaged was lack of skills had here been remedied. What was wrong? I left saying that I would think it over and get in touch as soon as I had something to recommend.

The answer came to me a short time later, back in Washington, while on the aforementioned bus ride. Workers on jobs were not just instruments using functional and specific content skills, but also people using adaptive skills. Adaptive skills were those competencies they needed to manage themselves in relation to conformity and change. And how did workers acquire these skills? They were acquired starting at the mother's breast and absorbed in the cultural context of growing up.

Working in white employment environments meant learning new ways of getting along other than the adaptive street smarts that worked in a different environment. This required a sensitive, tolerant environment that accepted you for who you were. That simply did not exist in most situations where Rev. Sullivan's trainees were placed. What was needed was sensitivity training both for whites and blacks so that adaptive skills could emerge and be reenforced. Adaptive skills involved a two-way street.

What are some of the Adaptive Skills? They include behavioral styles as they relate to, for example:

- Time, Space, Geography (getting to and from work).
- Moving toward, away from, or against people.
- Preferred Instructions (prescription/discretion mix).
- Impulse Control, control of self-gratification, expectations.
- Initiative, resourcefulness, direction of ambition.
- Dealing with authority.

Reviewing these, and the many more that could be added, it quickly becomes apparent that Adaptive Skills define who a person is, the kinds of things that a person has in mind when he or she says, "This is who I am!" Consciously or subconsciously a person looks over a specific employment situation and decides, "yes" or "no," whether it is suitable. They are not in the first instance thinking, "I am a machinist, a typist, a welder, or whatever." They are in the first instance thinking, "This is who I am! I think this situation I'm looking at will suit me. I'll do my machining, or typing, or welding here and give it a try." In short, Adaptive Skills are basic to an individual's choice process.

Systems Approach: Linking Behavior—Knowledges, Skills, and Abilities (KSAs)—Results

FJA is a systems approach. Systems involve a master purpose. All of the components of the system must be evaluated for their contribution to the master purpose. In FJA, the fundamental unit is the task, and it is expressed as a statement embodying a behavior moderated by KSAs leading to a result. The result is the purpose of the task. The result provides feedback to the behavior as to whether or not the performance standards are being achieved. Thus, a task statement is the fundamental unit of a work system. The purpose of a work system is achieved by clusters of tasks embodying technologies designed to achieve objectives and goals that add up to the purpose. In this sense the task is like a cell (a building block) in the human body.

What was the origin of this idea? It occurred to me when I was working at the aforementioned scientific research laboratory, which was a development center for missiles and satellites and was system driven. There my first approach to FJA data gathering had been self-reports consisting of functionally oriented checklist items along with lists of knowledge and special skills. These were quite long, consisting of several hundred items. When they were completed I was faced with a problem analogous to that confronting all checklist developers. I did not have a coherent, integrated picture of the job. I had to piece such a picture together from the bits and pieces of my self-report.

My clue for doing so was a brief open ended description the incumbent was asked to write at the beginning of the self-report. Essentially what everyone wrote was the driving purpose of their job, which was achieved by a whole series of results in turn achieved through the performance of individual tasks.

I pursued this observation through analysis of the self-reports and the marginal notes and comments of the incumbents. This made it possible to reconstruct the tasks, linking results to behaviors and specific KSAs. It was at that time the checklist was laid to rest and the system module was born.

The consequences of this change in approach were enormous. To begin with, I had found a way to establish the intrinsic validity of the tasks and thus the job analysis information. Behaviors, KSAs, and Results had to fit together like pieces in a jigsaw puzzle. Furthermore, the results had to add up, belong to the technology, and contribute to objectives in the form of tangible or intended outputs. The task bank had to make sense to incumbent and supervisor. It was now a picture in focus.

Incumbents could now use their own terms/jargon to describe what they were doing, but I could ask them to explain what they meant in relation to one or another part of the system module. It became almost impossible to pull the wool over my eyes. The fact that I could follow up what I was being told with pointed questions led some of the incumbents to believe I was really one of them, a ringer, in other words.

The FJA Focus Group Interview

The focus group interview grew out of observations that I am sure many of you have also made when doing job analysis. About 20 years ago I was employed to analyze the jobs of heavy equipment operators, members of the International Union of Operating Engineers. The purpose was to determine why they needed a 4-year apprenticeship to do their work. In the course of individual interviews (which were necessary because you cannot really know what a crane operator is doing by just observing him or her, although you can see what is getting done) I found many of the engineers were not very verbal about their work on a one-to-one basis.

Because many of these interviews were conducted on site, I frequently went out with the operators after work to a nearby pub to have a beer. In that situation, when a group of us sat together, the conversation typically was about the work, and the nonverbal engineers suddenly became not only verbal, but extremely verbal. I also noticed that in their conversations they both supplemented and corrected what they each had to say, often using very colorful language. I therefore proposed that we hold group interviews. This was agreed to despite the complicated arrangements sometimes involved. However, in the long run it saved time and produced more valid data. Oversights, exaggerations, insights all went through a leavening process in the group.

The basic format for an FJA interview is to ask the following five questions in sequence with appropriate follow-up to obtain specification, expansion, and clarification as necessary:

- What do you get paid for? (Outputs)
- What do you need to know to produce the Outputs? (Knowledges)
- What do you need to be able to do to apply those knowledges? (Skills and Abilities)
- What do you actually do to accomplish each of these Outputs? (Tasks)
- What standards, yours and your organization's, do you work to achieve? (Performance Standards)

Wherever possible I conduct group interviews with five or six incumbent "journeymen" having pretty much the same job title and definitely belonging in what management considers is the same job family. Management is not always right about the incumbents belonging to the same job family, and so I prefer to test the waters myself by reviewing existing information. I make mistakes, too. Supervisors are not included in these groups except under very special circumstances. In all cases I arrange for participants to receive an invitational letter from me that states the purpose of the job analysis (as worked out with management), describes the format of the 2-day interview, and invites their cooperation as Subject Matter Experts (SMEs)

The language and the tone of the letter is intended to reduce anxiety and allow the incumbents to question me in any way they like before the session begins.

One of the great advantages of the focus group is that the participants practically always have a good time and conclude by telling me how much they enjoyed the session and how much they learned about their job through the exchange that took place with their peers.

The FJA analyst is actually a facilitator. Aside from asking the questions noted earlier, he or she does not intrude with personal knowledge of the job under study. The analyst may, however, describe personal experiences as a facilitator, where they are relevant, and help to lighten the interview process.

Although I use the same format for individual interviews and for groups of two and three, it is not quite the same. Nevertheless, the results have been satisfactory. I recently did an entire social service agency where over three-fourths of the jobs had three or fewer workers. These interviews often take no more than a day.

FJA is a Holistic Concept

Although one of the original premises of FJA was that the whole person came to the job, not just an individual with certain instrumental skills, it nevertheless did not purport to be any more than a pragmatic approach to job description. It affirmed that workers related to Things, Data, and People and did so from simple to complex ways. It was kind of neat that these three classes of objects corresponded to what was measured in people by physical, mental, and interpersonal tests to establish their qualifications to meet job requirements. However, no more was made of it than that the correspondence occurred.

As I have already indicated, once I got out in the real world, my vision was forcibly enlarged. The limited view I had was really a phenomenon of the data in the DOT definitions, which was the source for all our research. I quickly discovered there was such a thing as Instructions the workers had to follow to fulfill the control standards of the organization they worked for. Some years later I further discovered, again in the real world of placement, that workers had to adapt to environmental factors in the work situation as well as to specific content. Together these two categories—Instructions and Environmental Factors—were a major challenge to a person's Adaptive Skills. My original idea of wholeness as represented by Things, Data, People and their counterpart Physical, Mental, and Interpersonal skills fell short of the wholeness that I had envisioned. My revised concept of wholeness was that of an individual in a social complex. The evolution of my thinking led me to a concept that John Dewey expressed over 100 years ago, namely, that it is a mistake to think of the individual as something separable from the social context in which he or she lived and worked. He wrote, "the non-social individual is an abstraction arrived at by imagining what man would be if all his human qualities were taken away" (Dewey, 1888).

Thus, my first intimation of holism was a recognition that FJA was not complete until it included in its conceptual scheme both Job Content as represented by Functional and Specific Content Skills and Job Context as represented by Adaptive Skills. And, as I noted earlier in my discussion of Adaptive Skills, this revised view of holism provided an understanding of the dynamics of job and career choice.

I have come to see the holistic aspect of FJA in another vital way; namely, that it can help us to understand Stress in the Work Situation and what to do about it. For the whole person to function optimally, to be fully productive, he or she must be in tune with with the job–worker situation.

The feedback from the job–worker situation must confirm that where the workers are working is where they want to be, that it suits their behavioral style. When it is confirmed, workers experience the positive stress that energizes them to excel, to use their functional potential to the utmost, to go through the roof as far as their special talents are concerned. If for some reason, either intrinsic to the job content or extrinsic relating to job context, workers feel they are not where they want to be or should be, negative stress occurs and barriers to productivity multiply. In the hundreds of focus groups I have conducted, the conditions for both positive and negative stress have always surfaced, particularly during the discussion of Performance Standards.

The sensitive, aware employer concerned about human resources and its contribution to productivity, as well as that of capital investment, knows this. In one way or another, employers listen with the third ear and act appropriately. Nowadays it involves hearing job-context matters such as sexual harassment, the problems of single parents caring for children, the needs of persons with disabilities, and the problems associated with shift work. Taking action in such matters, caring for workers as people, can go a long way in reducing negative stress and transforming it to positive stress.

Thus, indirectly , as it were, I arrived at a place I always wanted to be; namely, a place where somehow my moral and aesthetic values and my scientific research would meet. This they have done in FJA, particularly in its penetration to holism. Along with Huxley (1977)[2] I believe that "an ethic and a philosophy are very important in creating a suitable mental atmosphere in which we can act in the right way towards our natural surroundings…. We {also} need an aesthetic, an organized sensibility, which will polarize our feelings and thoughts in an artistic way towards the world" (p. 37). (He expressed these sentiments in 1959 during lectures at the University of California, Santa Barbara, 4 years before his death.)

SUMMATION

I trust the foregoing has given you a better idea than you may have had concerning the nature of FJA. I am grateful for the opportunity the preparation of this paper has given me to recall and relate the origins of FJA to its overrall practice. In my own mind I continue to be amazed at how much of what I have created has its roots in my parents, my teachers, my SMEs, and my management clients, who have challenged me with specific needs and problems.

More than ever I am aware that FJA is an organic whole, a living, growing, developing heuristic methodology. At present, I am preparing a

[2]Huxley, A. (1977). Ferruci, P. (Ed.), *The human situation*. New York: Harper & Row.

volume with my colleagues of benchmarks for every level of the functional scales to facilitate and expand the use of the scales for job evaluation purposes. In addition we are working on a structured interview for selection purposes. We think the FJA approach will help improve and validate this tool. Who knows what the future holds?

Appendix E: Application of FJA to Job Evaluation

EQUALITY AND FAIRNESS IN COMPENSATION

Perhaps nowhere in human resource management is the need for benchmarks more pressing than in job evaluation. The essence of job evaluation is having a common metric according to which all jobs can be valued and objective benchmarks to which all jobs can be compared to justify pay differentials. This is what this chapter is about. It provides a step-by-step procedure for applying FJA ratings to establish values for jobs so that all jobs can be compared with each other. The benchmarks in chapter 8 provide the anchors for the valuations.

Workers Need to be Paid Equitably and Fairly

After all is said and done to achieve productive efficiency and effectiveness in an organization through careful selection of suitable employees, design of jobs for smooth flow of work, and training that is directed specifically at performance, it can all fall apart through unwise and inadequate compensation of employees. Employees need to feel they are being dealt with equitably and fairly, both with regard to other workers in the organization and in comparison to workers outside the organization doing similar work. Nowhere is this manifested better than in their compensation.

Equitably in this context refers to work established to require "equal" or "similar" levels of skill, complexity and training. *Fairly* refers to the recognition of unique or exceptional factors in work situations either of a negative or positive nature. Thus, for two jobs otherwise judged to be equal, if one involves extreme negative environmental conditions of one sort or another (e.g., extremes of heat or cold or exceptional isolation), then fairness requires that the latter should receive a premium to compensate for the exceptional conditions that in effect make them unequal. The premium is an extra that should not disturb the already established status of the two jobs as being equal in skill, complexity, and required training.

TWO MAIN WAYS OF PAYING WORKERS

There are two main ways to pay workers fairly and equitably. They can be paid on the basis of the job, the job being ranked for level of difficulty or complexity in relation to other jobs. Or they can be paid on the basis of their personal skills, the more skills they bring to a job–worker situation, the more they will be worth. Both methods are influenced by the worth of the job or the skills in the marketplace.

There are advantages and disadvantages to both methods. The former is by far the most common, perhaps because it is the oldest. It has the advantage of being, or at least appearing to be, the most objective. It is based on job descriptions and these can be more or less agreed on by putting them in writing and negotiating their relative worth by what it takes to perform them satisfactorily. This includes education, training, experience, verbal, numerical, spatial relations abilities, and physical demands. The more (higher degree) of these factors required by a job, the more the job is considered worth for pay purposes. The disadvantage of this approach is that workers put forth in their jobs far more skill and effort than is rated in the job description. What is more, this approach tends to limit workers to their job description when the natural tendency of most workers is to grow in their jobs, go beyond its boundaries, and meet the challenges of the moment.

The latter method—paying the person—is not very common, although depending on how defined, surveys find the method in use in from 5% to 40% of large corporations (Lawler, 1990). It is especially associated with research and development endeavors, teamwork, participative management, and high technology organizations. The recent developments in the workplace of increased use of teamwork in a variety of industries as well as the expectation that workers be willing to perform a wider range of duties than those specified in job classifications written into negotiated contracts have had the effect of increasing the range of skills demanded in job–worker situations. Where such developments occur, workers are being paid increasingly on the basis of skill rather than job evaluation. A major disadvantage, nevertheless, is that paying workers on the basis of their skills presents significant problems in the definition of skills to be paid for and in administration.

FJA lends itself equally well to either approach. However, here we describe its application only to job evaluation, that is, the objective

---

Lawler, E. III. (1990). *Strategic pay.* San Francisco: Jossey-Bass.

establishment of the comparable worth of jobs. In FJA, all jobs are rated for the same range of factors and can all be given point values that in effect establish their relative difficulty or complexity.

Willingness to accept the idea that more complex jobs are by and large worth more money has more or less been ingrained in the American value system and appears to be widely accepted—so long as other contingent factors are also taken into consideration. Among these contingent factors that can receive special pay allowances but are not included in the ranking of the complexity of the job are: hazards, extreme working conditions (heat, cold, fumes), seniority, allowances for cost of living, family size, child care, education, training, and performance excellence (paid by bonus). Payment for these contingent factors is by no means universal and is frequently a matter determined by the culture, sometimes by legislation, and at other times as the result of collective bargaining.

FJA APPROACH TO SKILL EVALUATION: A FOUR-FACTOR APPROACH

FJA considers that a job, whatever its level of complexity, involves the whole person and therefore all aspects of a worker's involvement in the job should be considered in the compensation. Four types of factors contribute to this whole-person involvement: Functional, Holistic, Organizational, and Premium or Special Adaptation factors. The first three are intrinsic to the skill requirements of jobs and reflect the qualifications necessary to fulfill them, such as the individual's capacities, investment in self, and willingness to assume responsibility. They characterize jobs in their ordinary relation to each other. The Premium factors represent special adaptations individuals make to the environment in which jobs occur. They reflect ways in which workers are willing to extend themselves to adapt to the work situation.

These four types of factors will, upon close examination of the information represented by them, be found to correspond to the skill, effort, training, responsibility, and working conditions that are covered in traditional compensation plans.

The information required by the FJA job evaluation system is obtained by the use of the 10 measures already described (3 for skill level, 3 for orientation, 3 for Reasoning, Math, and Language, and 1 for Worker Instructions) and several additional scales that are very simple to use. Among them is a Strength Scale with values already supplied. A few of them, such as "consequences of error," require that values be established by the organizations using the system.

The ratings are made from the summary job description of a task bank designed to reflect the highest functional levels in each of the functional scales. For the present purpose we use a summary for a Home Security Technician, a job that occurs in the social service field in urban centers.

Summary Description for Home Security Technician

Cut materials, e.g. lexan (a transparent acrylic plastic), plywood, burglar and other metal bars, on power saw, following specifications and measurements on work orders prepared by supervisor; loads van with materials weighing up to 50 pounds including Kwik-Set Locks, jigs for locks, security pins, and hand and portable power tools; drives to clients following an itinerary determined by supervisor; greets client, describes purpose of visit, requesting dogs be leashed, and proceeds to install locks and other materials according to work order; uses a variety of tools, and on occasion when work order doesn't fit situation, makes a judgment call as to appropriate installation and fit of materials, drawing on brief training and knowledge of materials and relying on experience, skill with hand tools and interpersonal skills in order to make a secure installation and satisfy client.

The ten basic FJA ratings plus strength for this job are:

Level			Orientation				GED			
Things	Data	People	Things	Data	People	WI	Reas	Math	Lang	Str
3a	3b	2	3	1	2	2	3	3	3	3

These numbers are scale values and derive from the following analysis of the summary job description.

The orientation values tell us this is primarily a Things job, secondarily People, and thirdly Data. The orientation ranks reflect the following percentages that were assigned to these components: 60 15 25. These percentages were assigned to express the judgment that the Things performance standards were most important, the People standards next most important, and the Data standards the least important of the three.

The functional levels tell us that this job involves Manipulating (as it relates to tools and equipment), Computing (as it relates to the measurements that need to be made), and Exchanging Information (as it relates to establishing rapport with people on a service level).

The enabler abilities involve being able to follow instructions in which the worker has some leeway in the procedures and methods used to get the work done, common-sense understanding to carry out instructions where the work involves several concrete variables, ability to perform arithmetic calculations where dimensional specifications are marked on materials, and language ability sufficient to carry on ordinary conversations with customers, explain their work, and establish rapport. The strength rating, derived from Table 1, represents the lifting of 50 pound weights required by this job.

The ratings here and their interpretation follow from the earlier chapters in this document. These ratings are values that are entered in the places they are called for in the form shown in Fig. 1.

The presentation that follows will take the reader, in order, through the rationale of the use of the ratings as values for the aforementioned factors. The factors are represented in the four columns shown in Fig. 1. The method of calculation is illustrated by applying it to the Home Security Technician. In addition, the point values for a number of jobs in the same organization as the Home Security Technician are presented to provide a perspective of how certain selected jobs might line up in relation to each other.

Column 1: Functional Skill

This column has four sections, one each for Physical (Things), Mental (Data), and Interpersonal (People). The fourth section, involving an executive decision concerning organizational values, is discussed following a description of the calculations relating to the first three sections.

Each of the first three sections has a place for the ratings listed above for the Home Security Technician. Thus, under Physical, Things Level takes a 3 (see Table 1) for Manipulating; Strength (the enabler) takes a 3; and Orientation takes a 3. The formula for combining these values to obtain a subtotal is as follows: Level plus Enabler times Orientation = Subtotal. Substituting the figures in this formula, we obtain 3 plus 3 = 6, times 3 = 18.

Before we continue any further we need to explain the rationale for adding the enabler to the level and then multiplying by the orientation value.

Rationale for Adding Enabler Values to Level

Skill levels have as enablers physical, mental, and interpersonal factors appropriate to Things, Data, and People. Enablers are added to the functional level because they are considered as being complementary to the level, integral with the behavior.

Thus, in the case of Things, the significant enabler is active strength such as is involved in lifting, carrying, pushing, and pulling. There is a 5-point scale from Sedentary to Very Heavy to reflect different degrees of such physical involvement (see Table 1). It ranges from no significant weight manipulated to over 75 pounds handled with significant frequency. The appropriate scale value is added to the skill-level value before the effort multiplier is applied.

The enabler for data is reasoning and/or math. The one having the higher rating is used as the value for entry. The rationale for using one or the other as the enabler for the data function is that data requires mental

FUNCTIONAL FACTORS	HOLISTIC FACTORS	ORGANIZATIONAL FACTORS	PREMIUM FACTORS
Physical Factors	*Consequences of Error*	Number of Progrmas Managed	Extreme Work Conditions
Things level		Value of Programs Managed	Shift Work
+			
Strength		Number of Clients Served	Hazards
x			
Orientation			Overtime
=			
Subtotal:		Level of Persons Contacted	Isolated Location
Mental Factors			
Data Level		–Internal	Labor Market
+			
Reason/Math	Responsibility	–External	–Shortage
x	(Prescription/		
Orientation	Discretion)		–Surplus
=		Number of Persons Directly	
Subtotal:		Supervised	Merit Performance
Interpersonal Factors		Number of Persons Indirectly Managed	Cost of Living
People Level			
+			
Language			
x			
Orientation			
=			
Subtotal:	Specific Vocational Preparation (SVP)		
Relative Value Management Places on			
Things ———			
Data ———			
People ———			
Subtotal: SKILL	Subtotal: HOL	Subtotal: ORG	Subtotal: PRE

GRAND TOTAL:

FIG. 1. Functional job analysis format for job evaluation.

237

TABLE 1
Strength Scale

Physical Effort (Lifting)	Weight
Very heavy; over 75 pounds	5
Heavy: 50–75 pounds	4
Medium: 25–50 pounds	3
Light: 5–25 pounds	2
Sedentary —	1

activity to apply knowledge, and both reasoning and math are the appropriate mental activities for this component. Again, the reasoning and/or math are integral with the behavior. In most jobs, other than certain selected academic or scientific jobs, reasoning will have the higher rating and will be the one applied.

The enabler for the interpersonal function is language and the rating for language is its value. In the work situation, the most common form of interpersonal activity is by means of spoken language (accompanied, of course, by body language).[1] Written job orders may also be spoken, or, at any rate, elaborated on through the spoken word. The language scale provides speaking and reading illustrations. (When interpersonal activity occurs mainly through writing it is considered a data function and would be rated for the reasoning involved.)

Rationale for Using Orientation Value as a Multiplier

The orientation component is the source of the effort multiplier. It is not integral with the function as is the enabler; rather, it is a function of the demands of the work and the quality of the worker. The effort contributed to the function and enabler can increase productivity enormously, far beyond mere addition.

The reasoning is as follows: Effort applied for each task is total effort or 100%. However, the skilled worker gives each of the three functional components—Things, Data, People—the proportion of 100% that is warranted by the nature of the task to achieve the desired standards. The individual does this more or less unconsciously as a result of training and experience. (It is not unlike the feeling and tonal value that a concert violinist or pianist learns to give each note and phrase of a musical composition drawing on their training and personal experience.)

---

[1]If the language of communication is American Sign Language (ASL), then it is likely a physical level should be assigned to indicate the precision level involved.

Functional job analysts assign such proportional values on the basis of their understanding of the standards that need to be achieved in a given task. The proportional amount (the three proportions must, of course, add to 100) must be supported by data in the task statement and be acceptable to the incumbent.

(Although this rationale has been described in terms of tasks, the basic units of job–worker situations, the same rationale applies to the evaluation of the job summary in line with the orientation determination made earlier. The summary will have been written to reflect the highest functional levels of the job's tasks.)

The proportions are translated to multipliers of 1, 2, and 3 according to the rank order of the three orientations. These multipliers can be adjusted to higher figures, for example, 10, 20, 30, to obtain a greater spread of skill values. These larger numbers will not have any effect on the relative rank order of the skill subtotal for the particular job.

Following through for Mental in the same manner as was done for Physical we have the following numbers to substitute in the formula: Level—3 for Computing, Enabler (Reasoning or Math, whichever is higher—in this case both are the same)—3, Orientation—1. Combining these numbers in the previous formula results in a subtotal of 6.

In the case of Interpersonal, the numbers are: Level—2 for Exchanging Information, Enabler (Language)—3, Orientation—2. Combining these numbers in the formula results in a subtotal of 10 (2 + 3 times 2).

Relative Value of Things, Data, People Skills

The final item in the Functional Factors column—Relative Value Management Places on Things, Data, People—deals with an important management decision that needs to be made at the outset of the job evaluation process. The question is: Of the three, Things, Data, People accomplishments, which is most important to management in the given organization? What does management value most? Whatever it decides, it must apply the values arrived at in its decision to all the jobs in the plant. It cannot, in all fairness, shift its decision for the convenience or favor of a particular group of workers. If management decides that what it values most is Things, then Data, and then People, on the order of 7, 5, 3, and uses these weights to add to the component subtotals, it must stay with these weights for all the jobs in the organization. The addition of these weights is a way of bringing underlying beliefs to the fore and accounting for them by adding points to the basic skill total.

The organization employing the Home Security Technician is a community service organization dealing especially with the needs of the poor and providing them with social services. This organization values its relation to people highest, the data it collects on the basis of which it makes its decisions next highest, and the extent to which it deals with things least. It therefore assigned the following values to Things, Data, and People—2, 5, 7. What these figures are saying is the following: A person's ability to work with People is worth a bit more to us than three times their ability to work with Things, and their ability to work with Data is worth a bit more than twice as much as their ability to work with Things. (The numbers are arrived at by trial and error to reflect the dominant feelings expressed.)

Only one of these weights is assigned to a job, namely, the one that corresponds to the highest orientation of the particular job. Thus, in the case of the Home Security Technician which had as its highest orientation value Things, two (2) will be added to the subtotals of 18, 6, and 10 for an overall subtotal for the column of 36.

COLUMN 2: HOLISTIC FACTORS

Holistic factors are so named because they relate to the whole job. They underlie or overlay the whole person's functioning in the job. The three holistic factors are: Consequences of Error, Responsibility (as reflected in the execution of the prescriptive and discretionary aspects of instructions), and Specific Vocational Preparation (SVP). They cannot be expressed in terms of the analytic factors—Things, Data, and People.

Consequences of Error

Error results in losses. Losses can occur in material, money, staff time, morale, and organizational image. Losses occur because of ignorance (lack of training) failures in judgment, courtesy, and cooperation, and because of a lack of discipline in following the social and work rules relating to work behavior and time. The extent of the losses (expressed for the subject organization) can be:

HIGH	Affect the whole organization—give the organization a black eye and have a ripple effect in the community or marketplace. It could lead to bankruptcy or a tremendous uphill struggle to overcome the negative effects.
MEDIUM HIGH	Affect the organization in loss of significant financial support—for example, loss of a major account, funding, grant, and/or database, or disaffection of a segment of population served (loss of market share).
MEDIUM	Affect a program in loss of material, money, staff time, or harm to client.

TABLE 2
Consequences of Error

5	High	30	$50,000 +
4	Med-high	20	$20,000–$15,000
3	Medium	12	$5,000–$20,000
2	Med-low	7	$1,000–$5,000
1	Low	3	$0–$1,000

MEDIUM   Affect a department or work unit in loss of material,
LOW   money, staff time, or harm to client.

LOW   Affect an immediate work process in loss of personal
          and/or supervisory time needed to correct error.

These five scale values are simply indicative. They can be extended to as many as 10 with the placement of dollar values on them (see Table 2). The issues in defining values for this scale are: is there information available to make the judgment and can the judgments be applied consistently?

Needless to say, the organization needs to be aware of where and how losses can occur, which tasks in which jobs are thus vulnerable, and to take appropriate precautions in safeguarding against them. Such precautions can occur in hiring, training, design of the workplace, design of procedures (e.g., traffic, safety and security education, and signing). Sometimes losses can reveal significant management neglect and point to remedial measures. It is essential as part of each worker's training and induction into the organization that he or she be alerted to the potential consequences of error inherent in failure to perform according to training and orientation.

There is a Low consequence of error for the Home Security Technician, one that would not involve more than a loss of $1,000. This yields a score of 3.

Responsibility

In the view of FJA, responsibility ultimately is a matter of following instructions, being accountable for that which is prescribed and that which is discretionary. Every job, from highest to lowest, has a set of instructions. As noted earlier in higher level jobs, the instructions are heavily weighted in the direction of discretion or judgment. The lower the level of the job, the more it involves prescription, following standing operating procedures (SOPs). It must not be overlooked that even on the simplest level there are discretionary aspects to the job, and that even on the highest level there are prescriptive aspects.

Responsibility is a matter for the worker to effectively and efficiently mix the prescriptive and discretionary aspects of the job as they relate to the

TABLE 3
Worker Instruction Scale

Range	Weight
8	
7	
6	
5	30
4	20
3	12
2	7
1	3

culture (value, traditions) of the organization in order to achieve the required standards. It is easier to evaluate responsibility for following prescriptive instructions because they are specific and typically involve numerical (quantifiable) elements. (These quantifiable elements represent the distillation of much experience.) It is much more difficult to evaluate discretionary instructions because they have not yet been reduced to standing operating procedures. Nevertheless, judgments will be made. A caution to be observed is to treat errors and successes in the uses of discretion equally. A discretionary failure may be as much the fault of the person issuing the discretionary instruction as the person executing it.

The rating for worker instructions as defined in the Worker Instructions scale provides the basis for the weight assigned (see Table 3).

For the Home Security Technician, the Worker Instructions Level is 2. "Inputs and outputs, tools and equipment are all specified but the worker has some leeway in the procedures and methods used to get the job done. Almost all the information needed is in the assignment instructions. Production is measured on a daily or weekly basis." Level 2 yields a score of 7.

Specific Vocational Preparation

This factor places a value on the relevant preparation in experience and training that an individual needs to reach normal production (RNP) for a given job. (It is not intended to characterize the individual who may have more or less training than is needed for the job.) The scale for SVP is shown in Table 4. Certain conventions have been adopted in evaluating an individual's qualifications:

- A 4-year college education is valued at 2 years of vocational preparation, whether in English or engineering.
- A 2-year associate degree with vocational orientation is valued at 1 year of vocational preparation.

- A specific 6-month business (e.g., secretary) or vocational course (e.g., electronic technician) is given full value as 6 months of vocational preparation.
- A fully served apprenticeship to achieve journeyman status is valued as 3 years of vocational preparation.
- Internships are given full value for time involved, year for year.
- Experience background needs to be evaluated for relevance—on functional, specific content, and adaptive skill levels—and judgment calls made as to the time value that will be assigned.
- In general, level 7—2 to 4 years—is the level required to perform in a craft such as carpenter or plumber or entering professional occupation, such as teacher, accountant, nurse.

The Specific Vocational Preparation for the Home Security Technician is judged to require up to 30 days or level 2, which yields a score of 10. The addition of the three scores for this column—3, 7, and 10—yields a subtotal of 20.

TABLE 4
Specific Vocational Preparation (SVP): Experience and Training

Level		Weight
9	10 years +	50
8	4 years - 10 years	45
7	2 years - 4 years	35
6	1 year - 2 years	30
5	6 months - 1 year	25
4	3 months - 6 months	20
3	30 days - 3 months	15
2	Up to 30 days	10
1	Short demo	5

COLUMN 3: ORGANIZATIONAL FACTORS

These factors are a further elaboration of responsibility as they mostly and specifically apply to the management functions in the organization. About the only item among these factors that will apply to workers generally are Level of Persons Contacted, unless they have assigned functions in participative management.

These factors deal quite specifically with the management of money, plant and equipment, and persons. Each of the items can have its own scale and may require some definition in terms of dollar ranges or programs. Programs can also be understood as departments.

Judgment calls need to be made as to the number of points assigned to persons supervised directly versus persons managed indirectly. Typically supervision is a more direct and involved relationship with people.

Level of Persons Contacted

The assumption made is that the higher the level of person contacted the greater the responsibility and cost of error. Thus, a major difference between a low-level secretary and executive secretary may be chiefly in this factor. This assumption can be extended to all jobs, but is probably more evident in managerial jobs.

An example for a social agency along with associated weights as shown in Table 5:

TABLE 5
Level of Persons Contacted

Level	Weight
External	
Service providers, line to line, vendors	5
Clients	7
Program directors, community leaders, block clubs	10
Agency heads	15
Legislators	20
Power brokers	25
Internal	
Program or project directors	3
Interdepartmental	6
Executive staff	9
Agency board members	10
Board of commissioners	15

Number of Clients Served

Number of Clients Served is intended to reflect client load for those jobs having contact with a client either within the agency or external to it. The factors in this column that apply to the Home Security Technician are the Level of Persons Contacted and the Number of Clients Served. The former involves contact with the Program Director internally, which has a value of 3, and with Clients externally, which has a value of 7. The latter involves contact with couples and/or families at the residences serviced, which warrants a value of 2. The three values—3, 7, 2—add up to a subtotal score of 12 for this column.

Table 6
Number of Clients Served

Number of Clients	Weight
1	1
2–3	2
4–5	3
6+	5

Job Evaluation Score for Home Security Technician

The three subtotal scores—36, 20, and 12—added up yield a grand total score of 68.

PREMIUM FACTORS

As noted earlier, these are not factors that are appropriately woven into the point scores reflecting the functional and specific content skill requirements of jobs, the factors that order jobs relative to one another in a generally acceptable manner. The reason is that the factors call for special adaptations on the part of individual workers or organizations to contextual factors of jobs that are not necessarily associated with skill acquisition. Premium factors are of roughly three types:

1. Worker adaptation to extreme or hazardous working conditions calling for particular willingness on their part. This category includes shift work, overtime work, or work in isolated situations.
2. Employer adaptation to unique needs and labor market conditions causing shortages or surpluses for particular specific-content skills or employee willingness to adapt to very special conditions.
3. Employer adaptation to loyalty and meritorious performance that contribute to the employer's stability, profitability, and growth potential.

These factors need to be compensated for by bonuses or premiums tacked on to the base pay of a particular job. In this manner, the comparative status of the jobs based on skill can be maintained and compensation for special circumstances can be seen for what it is.

COMPARATIVE POINT VALUES FOR JOBS IN A SOCIAL SERVICE AGENCY

Table 7 shows the point values for an array of jobs in a social service agency selected to show the spread of scores calculated in the manner demonstrated for the Home Security Technician. That is its only purpose—to show the spread of scores. The scores cannot be truly understood without resort to the actual tasks included in the job descriptions which are not included in this publication. However, the jobs have also been selected so that titles more or less reflect common understanding of the tasks usually represented by them.

TABLE 7
Selected Job Titles in a Social Service Agency Arranged by Predominant
Involvement With Things, Data, People in Increasing Point Order

Things	Data	People
Food Service Aide 55	Typist 59	Receptionist 64
Home Security Technician 68	Payroll Technician 58	Community Worker I 69
Maintenance Technician 68	Central Files 62	Street Worker 79
Home Security Specialist 85	Accounts Payable 73	GED Technician 83
	Accountant 88	Case Manager II 90
	Planner 98	Social Worker 96
	Chief Accountant 125	AODA Counselor 100
	Controller 141	Director, Older Adult Programs 105
		Director, Family Crisis Center 120
		Executive Director 173

Selected Bibliography

The following selected articles describe Functional Job Analysis, and it's application, in additional detail.

Fine, S. A. (1955, Spring). Functional job analysis. *Personnel Administration and Industrial Relations*.

Fine, S. A. (1955, May). What is occupational information? *Personnel and Guidance Journal, 33*(9).

Fine, S. A. (1986). Job analysis. In R. Berk (Ed.), *Performance assessment: Methods and applications* (pp. 53–81). Baltimore: The John Hopkins University Press.

Fine, S. A. (1988). Functional Job Analysis. In S. Gael (Ed.), *The job analysis handbook for business, industry, and government* (pp. 1010–1035). New York: Wiley.

Fine, S. A. (1988). Human service workers. In S. Gael (Ed.), *The job analysis handbook for business, industry, and government* (pp. 1163–1180). New York: Wiley.

Fine, S. A. (1988). Heavy equipment operators. In S. Gael (Ed.), *The job analysis handbook for business, industry, and government* (pp. 1301–1310). New York: Wiley.

Fine, S. A., & Cronshaw, S. (1994). The role of job analysis in stablishing the validity of biodata. In G. S Stokes, M. D. Mumford, & W. A. Owens (Eds.), *Biodata handbook: Theory, research, and use of biographcal information in selection and performance prediction* (pp. 39–64). Palo Alto: Consulting Psychologists Press.

Myers, D. C., & Fine, S. A. (1985). Development of a methodology to obtain and assess applicant experiences for employment. *Public Personnel Management, 14*, 51–64.

Olson, H. C., Fine, S. A., Myers, D. C., & Jennings, M. C. (1981). The use of Functional Job Analysis in establishing performance standards for heavy equipment operators. *Personnel Psychology, 34*, 351–364.

Primoff, E. S., & Fine, S. A. (1988). A history of job analysis. In S. Gael (Ed.), The job analysis handbook for business, industry, and government (pp. 114–29). New York: Wiley.

The following sources describe the characteristics of the Worker Function scales as originally developed for the *Dictionary of Occupational Titles*.

Cain, G., & Green, B. F. (1983). Reliabilities of selected ratings available from the Dictionary of Occupational Titles. *Journal of Applied Psychology, 68*, 155–165.

Fine, S. A. (1955, October). A structure of worker functions. *Personnel and Guidance Journal*.

Fine, S. A., & Heinz, C. A. (1957, November). Estimates of worker trait requirements. *Personnel and Guidance Journal*.

Fine, S. A., & Heinz, C. A. (1958). The functional occupational classification structure. *Personnel and Guidance Journal, 34*(2), 66–73.

Geyer, P. D., Hice, J., Hawk, J., Boese, R., & Brannon, Y. (1989). Reliabilities of ratings available from the Dictionary of Occupational Titles. *Personnel Psychology, 42,* 547–560.

Interview with Ramin Jahenbegloo. (1992, May 28). *New York Review of Books,* p. 51.

Lawler, E. III. (1990). *Strategic pay.* San Francisco: Jossey-Bass.

Miller. A. R., Treiman, D. J., Cain, P. S., & Roos, P. A. (1980). *Work, jobs, and occupations: A critical review of the Dictionary of Occupational Titles.* Washington, DC: National Academy Press.

Mosel, J. N., Fine, S. A., & Boling, J. (1960). The scalability of estimated worker requirements. *Journal of Applied Psychology, 44,* 156–160.

Schmitt, N., & Fine, S. A. (1983). Inter-rater reliability of judgements of functional levels and skill requirements of jobs based on written task statements. *Journal of Occupational Psychology, 56,* 121–127.

Index

Work
  doing vs. getting done, 2–3, 221–222
  objects of work, 16–17, 222–223
Worker functions
  definition of level and orientation, 16–18
  ordinal nature of, 17–18
  scales
    comparison with classification scales, 207–210
    historical changes, 208–210
    summary chart of, 4
Worker instructions
  definition of, 129
  development of, 224
  illustrative tasks (benchmarks), 131–148
  and job evaluation, 241–242
  ordinal nature of, 22–23
  prescription and discretion, 22

and responsibility, 23
scale level definitions, 130–144, 201–202
Writing task statements, 29–41
  active voice, 33–34
  common problems with verbs, 35–37
  components
    action enablers, 38–39
    action verb, 33–37
    results of action, 39–40
  importance vs. relevance, 39
  question elements, 29–31
  relation of results to action verb, 40
  style guidelines, 33–41
  structuring action enablers, 38
  use of adverbs and adjectives, 40–41
  use of parentheses, 41
  use of slash, 34
  and worker function verbs, 34–35

Margin Index

To locate a particular item, bend book in half and follow margin index to page with black edge marker.